— Who do you think is right?
— Both are correct, but you don't have to listen to them.
— What are you talking about? What should the government do?
— Nothing. The economy will decide the minimum wage as it pleases.

They must be around here somewhere. But I can't find them.

— I want to buy some perfumes. Do you have any?
— We have various kinds of perfumes, and they're very cheap.
— Are they real?
— Sure, smell them. They're the same as the real ones.
— Why do you sell them UNDERGROUND?
— Because if we sell them ON THE GROUND, we'll be caught red-handed.

— I don't understand why your salary is 100 times higher than mine!
— Don't you think I work very hard?
— I don't think so. All you have to do is give us orders about what to do.
— You don't know my job. I'm always on a "MISSION IMPOSSIBLE."
— What's that?
— I must find ways to raise your productivity while lowering your salary. It's extremely difficult. That's why I'm entitled to such an astronomically high salary.

— Major New Edition —

Let's Talk BUSINESS

Written by Neal D. Williams

LSKOREA

Introduction

This discussion book has been written for English language students who wish to study contemporary business topics in English. The book considers a wide range of issues, from *accounting fraud* to *wealth inequality*, from *economic bubbles to employment discrimination*, from *infrastructure* to *unemployment*. Each unit is introduced with a topic preview, consisting of several thought-provoking questions. The preview is followed by an authentic model conversation in which two individuals discuss an aspect of the issue being considered in the unit. These conversations use idiomatic language, the same type of language that native speakers of English are likely to use. Next, there is a reading passage that provides an overview of the main ideas related to the issue. Every attempt has been made to use the most current information, statistics, and perspectives in the reading section. Key words and expressions are highlighted in the reading passage.

Following the reading passage, the key words and expressions are defined in easy-to-understand language. Each key word or expression is then used in a sentence in order to illustrate the meaning in context. As every student of the English language knows, an individual word can have numerous meanings, and common words can have uncommon meanings. Therefore, each word or expression that is defined in this book is given the proper definition that fits with the context of the reading passage. For example, the most common meaning of the word *count* is "to list or name numbers." However, *count* can also be used as a legal term meaning "a distinct, separate charge in a criminal indictment by a prosecutor." The latter definition is the only one that applies to the reading passage in this book, so that is the only definition that is cited.

After key words and expressions are defined, readers are given seven questions designed to provoke discussion. These questions are almost all questions of opinion, not questions of fact. In other words, students should feel free to express their own opinion since there is no right or wrong answer to the questions.

Finally, as an added bonus, each unit concludes with a "current hot topic." There is a short reading passage about a controversial aspect of the topic being considered in the unit, along with two discussion questions.

Dedication

This book is dedicated to my lovely wife and best friend, *Eunkyung Won*.

Suggestions to the Student

Carnegie Hall in New York City was opened in 1891 and is now one of the world's most famous concert halls. Every musician dreams of performing there at some point in their career. An old joke asks the question: "How do you get to Carnegie Hall?" The answer: "Practice, practice, practice!" Many students of the English language frequently ask their teacher a similar question: "How can I become a great English speaker?" The best answer is: "Speak, speak, speak!" Of course, you have to know some grammar and vocabulary, but once you have a reasonable knowledge of those aspects, your skill in speaking English will depend on how much time you spend actually using the language.

Studies have shown that English speakers can become fairly fluent in Spanish with about 600 hours of practice. The same is true of Spanish speakers who want to learn English. The amount of time needed is fairly low because English and Spanish are somewhat similar. However, if an English speaker wants to learn Korean, that learner will need to invest about 2,200 hours of practice in using the language, and the same is true for a Korean speaker who wants to learn English. The two languages are dramatically different in appearance, grammar, and pronunciation, so much more time is needed. If you want to become a skillful English speaker, you need to accumulate as much time as possible in actually speaking the language.

One easy way to build up time in speaking English is to enroll in an English conversation class. When you are in your class, you should speak as much as you can. It is important that you not worry about using the correct grammar; just keep speaking, and you will communicate. You will also, slowly but surely, improve your conversational skills. The people who have become fluent in English are no smarter than you. They just kept trying to use English and speaking as much as possible until they gained some level of fluency. You can do the same!

Suggestions to the Teacher

If you are an English language teacher, you are naturally interested in inspiring your students to speak English as much as possible. How can this goal be accomplished? Here are several practical suggestions. First, it is important to emphasize to students that the discussion questions written in this book simply provide an opportunity to express one's opinion. There is no right or wrong answer. Language experts say that one of the most important duties of a language teacher is to reduce anxiety in the classroom. Therefore, it is crucial to convince students that everyone's opinion is valid and important.

Second, because the aim of a language course is to get students involved in speaking the language as much as possible, it is better to use pair work than group discussions. When students are in groups, they may feel intimidated by more fluent speakers, and they will feel reluctant to speak. However, if they are working in pairs, they are conversing with a partner and have no choice but to speak. As they speak more with their partner, they will gain in confidence and fluency.

Third, teachers need to emphasize to students that simply trying to speak in English will help them achieve their goal of fluency. Of course, students will often experience some stress when trying to express their opinion in another language. They may feel as though their grammar and vocabulary are inadequate and that they should speak using only grammar that is completely accurate. Effective teachers will explain to students that it's necessary to feel some stress, but that's not anything to worry about. Students should just keep talking, using the vocabulary and grammar that they already know. Over time, they will improve in speaking, as well as in vocabulary and grammar.

Let's Talk BUSINESS
Table of Contents

Introduction_06

Suggestions to the Student_07

Suggestions to the Teacher_08

Issue-1	Minimum Wage_10		Issue-17	The Stock Market_74
Issue-2	The Underground Economy_14		Issue-18	Interest Rates_78
Issue-3	Migrant Workers_18		Issue-19	Exchange Rates_82
Issue-4	Employment Discrimination_22		Issue-20	Trade Wars and Free Trade Agreements_86
Issue-5	CEO Salaries_26			
Issue-6	Unemployment_30		Issue-21	Attracting Investment_90
Issue-7	Brand Power_34		Issue-22	Economic Development and the Environment_94
Issue-8	Internet Shopping_38			
Issue-9	Advertising_42		Issue-23	Demographics and the Economy_98
Issue-10	Wealth Inequality_46		Issue-24	Social Networking and Business_102
Issue-11	To Buy or To Rent?_50		Issue-25	Business Ethics_106
Issue-12	Debt_54		Issue-26	Security from Cyberattacks_110
Issue-13	Economic Bubbles_58		Issue-27	Infrastructure_114
Issue-14	Patent Wars_62		Issue-28	Ethical Investing_118
Issue-15	Artificial Intelligence_66		Issue-29	Mergers and Acquisitions_122
Issue-16	Accounting Fraud_70		Issue-30	The European Union_126

Appendix_130 / Discussion Textbooks from LIS KOREA_138

— Who do you think is right?
— Both are correct, but you don't have to listen to them.
— What are you talking about? What should the government do?
— Nothing. The economy will decide the minimum wage as it pleases.

Topic Preview:

Does your country have a minimum wage? Do you think the wage is high enough? What are the pros and cons of raising the minimum wage? Of course, raising the minimum wage will help workers make more money, but would increasing wages cause businesses to hire fewer workers?

Dialogue:

Ethan: Mia, you're from Canada, right?

Mia: Yes, I am.

Ethan: What is the minimum wage in Canada?

Mia: Well, the minimum wage is set by each province, so it varies, but the average is about US$8 per hour.

Ethan: I see. Well, there's a big debate going on in the U.S. right now about the minimum wage.

Mia: Yeah, I read about that. Senator Bernie Sanders wants to raise it to $15, right?

Ethan: Yeah, that's right, and a lot of people support that idea.

Mia: What about you? Do you think $15 per hour is reasonable?

Ethan: Yes, I do. Right now, it's only $7.25. That's just not enough.

Mia: I'm sure most workers agree with you.

Ethan: True, but unfortunately, most employers do not agree.

Minimum Wage

A minimum wage is the lowest amount of money that employers can legally pay their workers. The first modern minimum wage laws were passed in New Zealand in 1894, followed by Australia in 1896. These laws were passed in order to stop the exploitation of workers in sweatshops. Nowadays, more than 90% of all countries have minimum wage laws. In the European Union, 22 member states have national minimum wage laws. The other six member states depend on trade unions to set minimum wages through collective bargaining. On a global basis, the countries with the highest minimum wages per hour at present are Australia ($13.59), Luxembourg ($13.05), Monaco ($11.58), France ($11.03), and New Zealand ($10.96).

The current national minimum wage in the United States is $7.25 per hour, but for tipped employees, such as servers in restaurants, the minimum wage is only $2.13. However, individual states can choose to have a higher minimum wage. In Massachusetts, the general minimum wage is $11.00 per hour, but for tipped employees, the minimum wage is only $3.75. In California, the minimum wage for all workers, including tipped employees, is $10.50.

In the 2016 U.S. presidential race, the status of the minimum wage became a hot-button issue. The Democratic candidate, Hillary Clinton, wanted to raise the minimum wage to $15 per hour. However, the Republican candidate, Donald Trump, wanted to keep the minimum wage at the current level, which he claimed would help keep the U.S. competitive with other countries. Also, he said that the minimum wage was appropriate for entry-level positions.

Supporters of a high minimum wage argue that it removes financial stress on families, encourages people to get a higher education, which in turn will enable them to get better paying jobs. Above all, an increased minimum wage raises the poorest and most vulnerable classes in society above the poverty line. In contrast, opponents of high minimum wages claim that such wages actually increase poverty because employers may lay off or even sack unskilled workers. Also, high wages force employers to replace low-skilled workers with machines, such as self-checkout computers.

ISSUE 01 MINIMUM WAGE

Vocabulary & Expressions:

exploitation
*selfish use of others to achieve wealth or success
- The CEO built his business through *exploitation* of his friends.

sweatshop
*a shop employing workers for long hours under poor conditions and for very low wages
- The American shoe company was accused of using *sweatshop* labor in Asian countries.

trade union
*a labor union of workers in specialized fields; different from a union of general workers in an industry
- The Air Line Pilots Association is the largest *trade union* of pilots in the world.

collective bargaining
*the process by which employers and labor unions agree on wages, rules, and working conditions
- In some countries, public workers are not allowed to form labor unions and engage in *collective bargaining* with employers.

server
*a person who waits on tables; a gender neutral word for the old-fashioned terms *waiter/waitress*
- Nowadays, most educated people in the U.S. use the term *server* instead of waiter/waitress.

hot-button
*exciting strong feelings, emotional
- The question of same-sex marriage is a *hot-button* issue in some countries.

entry-level
*relating to a low-skilled job, where employees may gain experience or skills
- Most high school graduates have no specialized skills, so their first job is usually at an *entry-level* position.

vulnerable
*capable or susceptible of being physically or emotionally wounded or hurt
- Teenagers are more *vulnerable* to risky activities because they haven't fully matured.

poverty line
*a minimum income level used as an official standard for determining how many people live in poverty; also known as *poverty threshold*
- In 2015, the *poverty line* in the U.S. was $24,250 per year for a family of four.

lay off
*to dismiss employees because of lack of business
- The CEO announced that the company would *lay off* 100 workers because of difficult economic conditions.

sack
*to fire someone from a job
- Bob was always late for work, so his boss had no choice but to *sack* him.

self-checkout
*a system that allows customers to total their purchases and pay for them without using a cashier
- Most Walmart stores now offer *self-checkout* for customers who don't want to go through a traditional checkout line.

Let's Talk Business

Let's Talk Business

● Discussion Points:

1. What is the current minimum wage in your country? Do you think it should be increased, decreased, or kept at the same level?
2. Is the minimum wage a hot-button political issue in your country? Was this issue debated by politicians in the last election?
3. Are there any jobs in your country where the minimum wage does not apply? Do you think the minimum wage should apply to all jobs equally?
4. Does your country require employers to pay a higher wage to employees who work at nights, on weekends, and on holidays? Do you think those employees should receive higher wages?
5. Is it possible for parents to support a family if the parents only have minimum-wage jobs?
6. What punishment should a company receive if they are caught paying their employees less than the minimum wage?
7. Have you ever worked at a minimum-wage job? How would you describe that experience?

● Current Hot Topic: Increasing the Minimum Wage = Increasing Unemployment?

Critics of increasing the minimum wage claim that increases will have the undesirable effect of increasing unemployment. The City of Seattle provided a good opportunity to test that idea when, in 2014, the city passed a law that would gradually raise the minimum wage to $15, the highest minimum wage in the U.S. After the first raise, one study claimed that unemployment had increased. However, another study claimed the exact opposite. It seems unclear exactly what effects that raising the minimum wage will have on unemployment. However, one thing is clear: workers will earn more per hour with an increased minimum wage.

● For Further Discussion:

1. Do you think that increasing the minimum wage will increase unemployment in your country? Why or why not?
2. Many American parents believe that it's good for their teenage and college-age children to work in a minimum wage job in order to learn the discipline of hard work. Do you agree with that idea?

— I want to buy some perfumes. Do you have any?
— We have various kinds of perfumes, and they're very cheap.
— Are they real?
— Sure, smell them. They're the same as the real ones.
— Why do you sell them UNDERGROUND?
— Because if we sell them ON THE GROUND, we'll be caught red-handed.

They must be around here somewhere. But I can't find them.

Topic Preview:

Have you ever paid cash for an item, so the government would not know about your purchase? Have you ever bought a counterfeit item, for example, a fake Gucci handbag or Rolex watch? If so, you were participating in the underground economy. Should governments allow the underground economy to flourish, or should they shut down this unregulated market?

Dialogue:

Liam: Olivia, how do you like my new watch?

Olivia: Wow! That's a Rolex, right? They are so expensive! Did you get a raise?

Liam: Not at all. I just know where to buy things.

Olivia: Let me take a look at it. Hmmm...this is not a real Rolex!

Liam: How did you know?

Olivia: On a real Rolex, there is a tiny magnifying glass above the date.

Liam: Well, you caught me! I bought this fake watch in Hong Kong when I was on vacation.

Olivia: I thought so! You know you could get into trouble for that.

Liam: No one will ever know. I bought it just for fun anyway.

Olivia: Well, maybe I should report you to the customs department just for fun.

Liam: You're kidding, aren't you?

Olivia: Maybe, maybe not.

The Underground Economy

The term "underground economy" refers to a market whose transactions are somewhat hidden and often illegal. This type of market is also called a "black market," "clandestine market," or "shadow economy." Participants in this type of market try to avoid governmental rules and prohibitions. There is a wide range of products and services that are available in the underground economy. At one end of the spectrum, there are mom-and-pop operations that sell products, such as fruit and vegetables, on the street. Since such vendors deal in cold hard cash only, the government has no way of knowing if these sellers are reporting all of their sales and paying their fair share in taxes. Since they pay little or no taxes, these sellers can improve their bottom line.

At the other end of the spectrum, there are individuals who use the underground economy to sell something that is totally illicit. Such illegal activities include selling and buying illegal drugs, smuggling endangered animals and selling them as pets or to be used in traditional medicine, and reproducing and selling copyrighted media without permission. The latter category of products includes DVDs of films, music CDs, computer software, and video games. Hollywood producers claim that they lose billions of dollars each year due to the sale of pirated media in South America and Asia.

Governments dislike the underground economy because its existence makes it difficult for governments to get a handle on the country's total economy. The government wants to have an accurate record of the nation's gross domestic product, so they can understand where the economy needs improvement. Therefore, the government will often offer incentives for citizens to report their income honestly. For example, the Republic of Korea allows citizens to pay less in taxes if they report their total credit card charges and total amount of cash purchases on their yearly income tax report.

ISSUE 02 THE UNDERGROUND ECONOMY

Vocabulary & Expressions:

clandestine — *done secretly, especially for purposes of deception
- The politician held a *clandestine* meeting in order to get a bribe.

spectrum — *a broad range of related ideas or objects
- The *spectrum* of political beliefs ranges from very conservative to very liberal.

mom-and-pop — *relating to a small business, usually owned and operated by family members
- My parents ran a *mom-and-pop* store, and I had no choice but to work in the store.

vendor — *a person who sells something (related to the word *vending machine*)
- There are many *vendors* of fruits and vegetables at our local open market.

cold hard cash — *cash in the form of coins or bills
- The seller would not accept credit cards; he wanted only *cold hard cash*.

pay one's fair share — *pay the amount that is appropriate for oneself
- The rich pay a lot of taxes, and the poor pay a small amount of taxes, but everyone should *pay their fair share*.

bottom line — *the last line of a financial statement, where the net profit or loss is shown
- The electronics company's new smart phone has become very popular, so it has improved the company's *bottom line*.

illicit — *not legally permitted, unlawful, or simply disapproved by society
- The businessperson rejected the bribe and said, "I will not participate in any *illicit* act!"

smuggle — *to take an item secretly in violation of the law
- The prisoner's friend *smuggled* a gun into the jail inside a cake.

copyrighted — *protected by exclusive right to make copies of an artistic work; also written as *copyright*
- You cannot photocopy this book because it is *copyrighted*.

pirated — *produced without permission or legal right
- You can find many *pirated* goods in the city's traditional market.

get a handle on — *to get an understanding or knowledge about something
- It took me a long time to *get a handle on* what my new boss expected.

gross domestic product — *the monetary value of all good services produced yearly in a country; often abbreviated as GDP
- The U.S.A. has the world's largest *gross domestic product*, but the EU is a close second.

incentive — *something that is used to motivate someone to make a greater effort
- The boss offered a bonus as an *incentive* to any employee who would quit smoking.

Let's Talk Business

Let's Talk Business

Discussion Points:

1. Do you think the government should try to shut down the entire underground economy, or should some parts of it be allowed to continue?
2. How extensive is the underground economy in your country? What are different types of the underground economy where you live?
3. In your country, what is the punishment for sellers who do not report their total income? Must they pay fines, go to prison, or do both? Do you think the punishment is appropriate?
4. What is the current GDP of your country? How much would the GDP increase if the underground economy were completely eliminated?
5. How widespread is the illegal drug trade in your country? Do you think people who are convicted of selling illegal drugs should suffer the death penalty?
6. Have you, or someone you know, ever bought a fake product? What name brand did the item represent?
7. Have you, or someone you know, ever photocopied an entire book? What sort of punishment would you have received if you were caught?

Current Hot Topic: Illegal Organ Trade

The term "organ trade" refers to the commercial trade of human organs, tissues, or other body parts for the purpose of transplanting them into another person. At present, the global need for healthy body parts far exceeds the numbers available. Even in advanced countries, many medical patients must wait over three years for an organ to become available. Commercial trade of human organs is illegal in most countries, so a black market exists where poor people sell a kidney or other tissues for a profit. Australia and Singapore have now legalized financial payments for living organ donors. Most other countries prohibit such a transaction.

For Further Discussion:

1. Should your country allow financial payments to living donors of human organs? Why or why not?
2. Would you ever donate an organ, such as a kidney, to help another person? Who would you be willing to help?

I'm from Mexico and work in the United States. I'm so proud of myself because I'm helping grow the US economy.

I'm from Korea and work in Australia as a welder.

I'm from India and am a software engineer. I contribute to the Canadian IT industry.

Some countries need migrant workers to make up for the lack of local workforce. They are the engine of the world economy. Foreign workers should be treated equally and fairly by law. They shouldn't be discriminated against for any reason.

Topic Preview:

Is it a wise decision for a nation to become a host country for migrant workers who come to live and work? Don't foreign workers take away jobs that should go to citizens? If we do allow foreign workers to enter the country, should we restrict their work opportunities to the worst types of jobs, tasks that citizens refuse to do?

Dialogue:

Sophia: Mason, you're from the U.S., right?

Mason: Yes, I am. Why do you ask?

Sophia: Well, I heard that the American president is going to limit the number of foreign workers entering the country.

Mason: He did say that. However, it's not clear if he's truly serious about it.

Sophia: What do you mean?

Mason: Well, I just read that the U.S. government agreed to allow 15,000 low-paid, seasonal workers into the country.

Sophia: I see. Well, what about workers with high-tech skills?

Mason: Silicon Valley wants to hire more of those because they can't find American workers with the necessary skills.

Sophia: I guess it's a lot more difficult to get along without foreign workers than people think.

Mason: Yeah, I agree. Sometimes, you need foreign workers because your own citizens can't do everything.

Migrant Workers

The term "migrant worker," or "foreign worker," usually refers to a person who leaves their home country in order to work in another country. It is estimated that more than 230 million migrant workers are currently working outside their home country. Migrant workers often do seasonal work. For example, in California, most of the work of picking fruit is done by migrant workers from Mexico. After the fruit season has ended, the workers return to Mexico. People sometimes refer to hard jobs such as fruit picking as "3-D jobs," meaning "dangerous, difficult, and dirty." Workers from poor countries are often willing to take such jobs, and they only want an honest day's pay. In advanced countries, most residents, who are well-educated, would not think of working on a 3-D job.

Another type of migrant worker is the person with high-tech skills. The United States allows American companies to hire foreign workers in specialty occupations that involve advanced knowledge in such fields as architecture, biotechnology, chemistry, engineering, mathematics, medical science, and other fields. These foreign employees are admitted into the U.S. on an "H-1B visa." If such workers quit their job or are fired, they must return to their home country, or they may be caught and forcibly repatriated. In 2015, there were more than 300,000 applicants for the H-1B visa, of which almost 80% were approved. Migrant workers who live for long periods of time in another country are often called expatriates, or expats.

Besides the millions of migrant workers who move to other countries legally, there are millions who enter another country illegally. These workers are often called "illegal aliens," but nowadays, most educated people prefer to describe them with the euphemism "undocumented workers." Many citizens resent the presence of foreign workers in their country, whether the workers are legal or illegal. The citizens may have a legitimate complaint, or they may simply be xenophobic. Such angry citizens often call for migrant workers to be sent packing.

ISSUE 03 MIGRANT WORKERS

Vocabulary & Expressions:

migrant
*a person who moves from place to place, especially to another country.
- In Canada, most agricultural work is now done by *migrant* workers from Guatemala.

seasonal
*to accompany the seasons of the year or some particular season
- Many American stores hire extra short-term *seasonal* workers for the Christmas season.

honest day's pay
*a phrase from the expression "an honest day's work for an honest day's pay." The saying means that, if you work faithfully, your employer will pay you faithfully.
- The boss said to his new employee, "If you put in an honest day's work, you will get an *honest day's pay*."

would not think of
*a strong way of saying that you would never consider taking a certain action
- The student told the teacher, "I *would not think of* cheating on a test!"

repatriate
*to bring or send back a person or refugee to their home country
- Ten undocumented workers were caught working on a farm, and they were immediately *repatriated*.

expatriate
*someone who leaves his home country to live and work in another country; abbreviated as *expat*; not to be confused with *ex-patriot*, a person who no longer feels loyal to his home country
- Korea has over 30,000 *expatriates* working as English teachers.

alien
*a foreign person. Nowadays the term is used mostly in governmental documents and sounds offensive if used in conversation with a foreign worker.
- Every English teacher working in Korea must have an *alien* registration card.

euphemism
*The use of a nice term instead of an offensive or hard term
- The expression "to pass away" is a common *euphemism* for "to die."

undocumented
*lacking the proper documents or paperwork needed to live or work in another country
- An *undocumented* student was discovered at my high school, but the school let her finish the school year.

resent
*to feel displeasure or indignation at a person or situation because you feel insulted
- Older workers often *resent* young supervisors who try to tell them how to do their job.

xenophobic
*fear or hatred of foreigners or people who are culturally different
- Politicians who talk about getting rid of all foreign workers are often said to be *xenophobic*.

send packing
*to dismiss and send away in disgrace
- The employee was caught stealing, so the boss *sent* him *packing*.

Let's Talk Business

Let's Talk Business

Discussion Points:

1. How many migrant workers are currently in your country? What countries are they usually from? Do they work mostly on 3-D jobs, or are some of them high-tech workers?
2. Have any politicians in your country ever talked about getting rid of most foreign workers? Were those politicians popular because of that sort of message?
3. Are there many undocumented workers in your country? What happens to them if they are caught?
4. Do you believe that undocumented workers in your country steal jobs that citizens would normally do? Why or why not?
5. Do you personally know any migrant workers in your country? What are their lives like? Are they ever mistreated by their supervisors?
6. If your country suffered from a low birth rate, would you support increasing the number of migrants as a way to increase the number of citizens? Why or why not?
7. Would you ever consider working on a 3-D job in your country or another country?

Current Hot Topic: Human Trafficking

Human trafficking refers to the trade of humans, most commonly for the purpose of forced labor. Migrant workers, especially undocumented workers, are vulnerable to human rights abuses and may end up being victims of human trafficking. According to experts, the human trafficking industry generates an estimated $150 billion in profits every year, much of which is earned in industrialized countries. In 2012, the International Labour Organization (ILO) estimated that 21 million victims of human trafficking were trapped in modern-day slavery.

For Further Discussion:

1. Is human trafficking a problem in your country? What types of jobs are trafficked people involved in?
2. If you discovered a worker in your country who was involved in forced labor, what would you do? Would you help them escape, or would you call the police?

Topic Preview:

If you started your own company, what sort of hiring practices would you follow? Would you hire an equal number of men and women employees? Would you hire a person from a racial minority? Would your hiring decisions be influenced by a person's age, color, religion, sexual orientation, or gender identity? Do your country's laws prohibit discrimination based on those factors?

Dialogue:

Ava: Jacob, I'm thinking about working abroad as an English teacher.

Jacob: Really? What made you decide to do that?

Ava: Well, I have a friend who did it for a few years, and she enjoyed it.

Jacob: Yeah, I've heard similar stories. Also, it can help you pay off student loans.

Ava: That's another reason why I'd like to take that job.

Jacob: Did you major in English?

Ava: Yes, I did. I majored in English literature. I also took some linguistics courses.

Jacob: That sounds great, but I have to caution you about one thing.

Ava: Yeah, what's that?

Jacob: Well, you are African-American, and it seems that some countries prefer white teachers.

Ava: Yeah, I know that, but there must be a place for me.

Jacob: True, but maybe you'll have to look for a while. Well, good luck in your job search!

Ava: Thanks!

Employment Discrimination

Employment discrimination is a form of discrimination that may be based on race, gender, religion, national origin, physical disability, mental disability, age, sexual orientation, gender identity, or pregnancy. The practice is sometimes called "workplace discrimination." If you apply for a job in the United States, you will likely read a "non-discrimination statement" on the job application form. Any employer who is caught discriminating against employees or job applicants is subject to massive fines and may be forced to pay both compensatory damages and punitive damages to the person who has been discriminated against. It is also illegal to retaliate against a job applicant or employee who complained about discrimination or filed a charge of discrimination.

Real-life examples of employment discrimination abound. An airline's job advertisement suggests that applications by young women in their 20s and 30s would be preferred. An employer decides not to hire a young woman when he hears that she's been married for two years and might have a baby. In fact, there is an entire series of questions that are illegal for employers to ask job applicants. These would include the following: Do you like to drink socially? How did you get that scar (or other physical abnormality)? What religious holidays do you observe? Who will take care of your children while you are at work?

Employment discrimination can occur even after a person is hired for a job. For generations, women have complained that they are not paid the same as their male colleagues. Statistics for 2015 showed that, in the United States, women earned about 83% of what men earned when working in the same position. Women also have a legitimate complaint about the glass ceiling. In 2016, only 4% of CEOs of Fortune 500 companies were women. Thus, many women work for peanuts and are stuck in a dead-end job.

Age discrimination is also widespread. However, in American society, there are elderly people who are still working. In 2016, there was a school teacher who was 102 years old, and Walmart had a 103-year-old employee.

ISSUE 04 EMPLOYMENT DISCRIMINATION

Vocabulary & Expressions:

discrimination
*positive or negative treatment of a person because of the group, class, or category to which they belong
- The apartment building owner was accused of *discrimination* because he refused to rent an apartment to a black person.

compensatory damages
*legal term for money awarded to a plaintiff that is equal to the amount that he lost due to the defendant's actions
- The teenager had to pay *compensatory damages* equal to the cost of a new window to replace the one that he accidentally broke.

punitive damages
*legal term for extra money awarded to a plaintiff because the defendant was reckless in his actions and should be punished
- A judge required that Exxon pay $2 billion in *punitive damages* because of their oil spill.

retaliate
*to do something bad to a person because they did something bad to you
- The boy played a trick on his sister by hiding her favorite sweater; however, she *retaliated* by hiding his favorite video game.

file a charge
*to sign documents with a court or legal authority accusing a person or company of wrongdoing
- The worker *filed a charge* of age discrimination with the National Labor Board because his company fired him when he reached age 70.

real-life
*existing or happening in reality
- Racial discrimination is not just something you see in fictional movies; it is a *real-life* problem faced by many people.

scar
*a mark left by a wound, sore, or burn
- I still have a *scar* on my knee from when I fell off my bicycle at age 9.

abnormality
*a condition, state, or situation that is different from what we normally expect
- His left arm was partially paralyzed, but he successfully hid this *abnormality* from most people.

glass ceiling
*an upper limit to professional advancement placed on women, minorities, and other groups
- Hillary Clinton lost her race for president, so the presidential *glass ceiling* has not yet been cracked in the U.S.

Fortune 500
*an annual list made by *Fortune* magazine that ranks the 500 largest U.S. corporations
- The number one company on the 2016 *Fortune 500* was Walmart, which had revenues of $482 billion for the year.

work for peanuts
*receive a small amount of money for your work
- If you don't want to *work for peanuts*, you'd better get a college education.

dead-end
*having no possibility for progress or advancement
- No one has been promoted in my company in 10 years; I think I have a *dead-end* job.

Let's Talk Business

Discussion Points:

1. What are the laws in your country concerning employment discrimination? Are those laws the same as in the United States?
2. Are there any job interview questions in your country that would be illegal? Why are they illegal?
3. Does your country have forced retirement for certain professions (e.g., teachers and professors)? Do you agree that forced retirement is a good idea for some jobs? Why or why not?
4. Many countries in Asia have a Confucian background, where elderly people are treasured for their wisdom, yet some of those countries require forced retirement for certain jobs. Isn't it a contradiction of Confucian values to force people to retire because of age?
5. Have you ever read about any lawsuits being filed in your country because of employment discrimination? What happened?
6. Do you think there is a glass ceiling in your country for women and minorities? Why or why not?
7. Have you, or someone you know, ever been discriminated against? What happened?

Current Hot Topic: Employment Discrimination Based on Sexual Orientation

The laws regarding sexual orientation vary greatly across the world. At one extreme, there are countries like Saudi Arabia, where same-sex romantic activity is punishable by imprisonment. Of course, in such conservative countries, there are no laws protecting LGBT people from employment discrimination. At the other extreme, there are countries like Denmark, which was the first country in the world to legalize same-sex unions, in 1989. Naturally, Denmark bans all anti-gay discrimination, including in the area of employment.

Note: LGBT = lesbian, gay, bisexual, transgender

For Further Discussion:

1. Does your country have laws that prohibit anti-LGBT discrimination concerning employment? Would you favor the enactment of such laws? Why or why not?
2. Who are some famous LGBT people in your country? What sort of jobs do they have? Do you think they have ever been discriminated against?

— I don't understand why your salary is 100 times higher than mine!
— Don't you think I work very hard?
— I don't think so. All you have to do is give us orders about what to do.
— You don't know my job. I'm always on a "MISSION IMPOSSIBLE."
— What's that?
— I must find ways to raise your productivity while lowering your salary. It's extremely difficult. That's why I'm entitled to such an astronomically high salary.

Topic Preview:

Do you think that CEOs are really worth their multi-million dollar salaries? Should their salaries be limited to a fixed multiple of the average worker's salary? For example, if the average worker earns $50,000 per year, should the CEO's salary be limited to five times that amount ($250,000), ten times ($500,000), or twenty times ($1,000,000)? Do workers have a right to complain about their CEO's huge salary?

Dialogue:

Aiden: Hey, Elizabeth! How about joining me for an ice cream cone at Ben & Jerry's?

Elizabeth: Oh, that sounds good, thanks! Is there a Ben & Jerry's shop near here?

Aiden: Yeah, there's a new one inside the Main Street Mall.

Elizabeth: Okay. I'll be ready in a few minutes.

Aiden: By the way, did you know that the founders of Ben & Jerry's limited their salaries for many years?

Elizabeth: What do you mean?

Aiden: They had a rule that the CEO's salary would never exceed five times the salary of entry-level employees.

Elizabeth: Wow! That's amazing! I've never heard of that.

Aiden: Yeah, it was a great policy from 1978 to 1995.

Elizabeth: What happened to change the policy?

Aiden: Well, Ben and Jerry searched for a new CEO in 1995, and they ended the five-to-one-ratio policy at that time.

Elizabeth: Still, that's incredible that they were able to maintain the policy for so long.

CEO Salaries

Among the largest corporations in the U.S., the CEOs earn an average of 300 times more than their workers, according to data from the Economic Policy Institute. Only 50 years ago, the ratio was about 20-to-1. In fact, the 200 most highly compensated American CEOs receive an average annual pay package worth more than $20 million. In 2016, Tom Rutledge of Charter Communications was the highest paid CEO, with a salary of $98 million. Les Moonves of CBS raked in about $70 million, and Bob Iger of the Walt Disney Company earned $41 million.

Students of business will remember the name of Jack Welch, who served as CEO of General Electric for 20 years. He excelled as a management guru and successfully maximized the company's revenue many times over. When he retired in 2001, the company awarded Welch with a severance package of $417 million, the largest payout in history.

Who is to blame for such outrageous salaries? People usually point the finger at the board of directors. Board members are usually highly paid themselves, so they naturally approve large pay packages. They also employ compensation consultants as hired guns, who compare pay packages at other firms and offer suggestions. To most outsiders, this approach will look like cronyism and inadequate corporate governance.

In 2017, French economist Thomas Pitketty published his magnum opus, *Capital in the Twenty-First Century*. He argues that the current glut of excessive CEO salaries can be traced to the American tendency to embrace the notion of superstardom or super-leadership, an idea that leads to the lionization of CEOs, celebrities, and athletes. This American propensity seems to rest on the "Great Man Theory," a 19th-century idea which states that history can largely be explained by the appearance of highly influential individuals. If the theory is true, then super-CEOs must deserve super-salaries. However, many people, especially workers, think that CEOs are only part of the formula of success. Corporate success depends on many people working together as a team, and all workers should receive their fair share.

ISSUE 05 CEO SALARIES

Vocabulary & Expressions:

pay package — *the total amount of compensation received by a worker, including salary, company stock, vacation time, and other benefits
- The company increased the CEO's total *pay package* because the company had doubled its profits during the previous year.

rake in — *to gather or collect in large quantities
- Because of the success of its iPhone 7, Apple *raked in* huge profits.

guru — *a leader or expert in a particular field
- Many businesspeople want to hear Philip Kotler speak because he has long been regarded as a *guru* of marketing.

many times over — *multiple times; again and again
- Bill Gates is a billionaire *many times over*.

severance — *money paid to employees who leave a job because of retirement or because of reasons beyond their control
- When Carly Fiorina was fired as CEO of Hewlett-Packard, she still received *severance* pay of about $100 million.

outrageous — *passing reasonable limits; intolerable or shocking
- During the tourist season, the resort hotel raises its prices to *outrageous* levels.

point the finger at — *to accuse someone of a misdeed
- The boy denied that he broke the window and instead *pointed the finger at* his brother.

board of directors — *an official group of persons who direct or supervise the activity of a company or organization, including the hiring of the CEO
- The university's *board of directors* just voted on the hiring of a new president.

hired gun — *a person hired to resolve disputes or to handle complex legal or business problems
- The company used *hired guns* to deal with the fired employees.

cronyism — *the practice of favoring one's close friends, especially in politics and business
- After the new president hired his best friends as government employees, citizens accused him of *cronyism*.

magnum opus — *a masterpiece or greatest work, a term often used of the most important work of an artist, musician, or writer
- Many people claim that the film *Titanic* was James Cameron's *magnum opus*.

glut — *an excessive supply or amount
- Hollywood produces a *glut* of films each year, usually more than 700.

notion — *an idea or conception, often one that is unproven
- The constant marketing of new smart phones is built on the *notion* that customers will always want to upgrade.

lionization — *the treatment of a person as a celebrity
- The *lionization* of employees who never take a vacation ends up creating an oppressive culture of overwork.

propensity — *a natural inclination or tendency
- Some people are born with a *propensity* for leadership.

Let's Talk Business

Let's Talk Business

● Discussion Points:

1. Do you think the American CEOs who are given such huge salaries deserve that money? Why or why not?
2. Are CEOs in your country generally paid huge salaries, such as 200 or 300 times what the average worker earns?
3. Who are the highest paid CEOs in your country? Do you think that they deserve their high salaries?
4. Do you agree with the "Great Man Theory," the view that history can largely be explained by the influence of a small number of powerful individuals?
5. Do you think that CEOs should be paid based solely on how profitable the company is? Why or why not?
6. Do you know of any companies in your country where the CEO has voluntarily limited his salary?
7. If you were hired as the CEO of a successful company, would you voluntarily limit your salary? What sort of limit would you choose: five times the average worker's salary, ten times, twenty times, etc.?

● Current Hot Topic: Government Intervention in Salary Ratios

In December 2016, the city council of the U.S. city of Portland, Oregon, voted to impose a special tax on companies whose CEOs earn more than 100 times the median pay of their average worker. Under the new rule, companies must pay an additional 10% in taxes if their CEOs receive compensation that is greater than 100 times the average pay of all their employees. Companies with CEOs who earn more than 250 times the median pay will have to pay a special tax of 25%. Portland's new regulation is the first time that a governmental body in the U.S. has passed legislation seeking to limit CEO salaries.

● For Further Discussion:

1. Do you think the government should intervene and limit the amount of CEOs' salaries? Why or why not?
2. Would you support a rule like the Portland regulation in your country? Why or why not?

— It's been three years since you graduated from college, and you still don't have any job. What's wrong?
— I've been looking for jobs that suit me, but I can't find one.
— What kind of job do you want?
— I don't want a six-digit salary job, but my working time should be FLEXIBLE. So I can work when I feel okay but stay home when I don't.

Topic Preview:

Does getting a college education mean that you will definitely be able to get a job in your field? Do recent college graduates in your country find it easy or difficult to get a job? If a person loses his job while in his 50s, can he easily get another job in his field? Does the leader of a democratic country actually have the power to improve the employment situation?

Dialogue:

Scarlett: Gabriel, it's been four months since I graduated from college, and I still don't have a job.

Gabriel: I'm sorry to hear that, but I'm not doing much better.

Scarlett: What do you mean? At least you have a job.

Gabriel: Well, I majored in business administration, but I'm now working at Starbucks. That's not exactly the type of work I envisioned for myself.

Scarlett: At least you're making some money.

Gabriel: True, but I make just enough to pay the bills while I keep looking for a better job.

Scarlett: Well, in my case, I think I'm going to have to take a simple job like working in a restaurant.

Gabriel: Well, I would recommend that. At least you can earn some money while you search for a job in your field.

Scarlett: I wish the college had told us it was going to be this hard to find a job before we paid all that money to get an advanced education.

Gabriel: Well, I think the economy has gotten worse in the past four years.

Scarlett: Yeah, you're right about that.

Gabriel: We just have to keep looking and remember the words of Winston Churchill: "Never give up!"

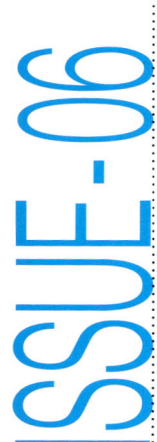

Unemployment

The unemployment rate is one of the crucial factors in determining the economic health of any nation. However, the methods of calculation of the unemployment rate vary from country to country. In order to compare unemployment rates fairly, the International Labour Organization (ILO) uses harmonized values. Unfortunately, some countries are years behind in reporting their unemployment rate, so statistics are often outdated. One recent chart of various nations showed a high unemployment rate of 95% in Zimbabwe (2009) and a low of 0.4% in Qatar. Other unemployment rates included the following: Singapore, 2.2%; Japan, 3%; the United Kingdom, 4.3%; the United States, 4.4%; South Korea, 4.9%; Australia, 5.8%; Canada, 6.6%; and Greece, 21.2%.

The long-term effects of unemployment are varied. High and persistent unemployment has a negative effect on economic growth, drives people into poverty, erodes self-esteem, and leads to social dislocation, unrest, and conflict. In the case of unemployed individuals, they may be unable to earn enough money to meet financial obligations. This lack of money may, in turn, lead to foreclosure on their mortgage and eviction from their home. Widespread unemployment leads to homelessness and may generate tent cities, which create another social problem for city officials to deal with.

Unemployment also affects people's health. Unemployed people have greater susceptibility to cardiovascular disease, depression, and suicide. In addition, they have higher rates of tobacco use, alcoholism, and drug use. Studies have shown that even people who generally have a sunny disposition find it difficult to look on the bright side of life when they are unemployed. Also, people who are highly conscientious suffer twice as much as others when they become unemployed. Research has also shown that the divorce rate is higher among couples when one partner is unemployed. Furthermore, high unemployment leads to a higher crime rate.

Governments use various measures to assist the unemployed. Benefits for the unemployed include direct payments, supplemental income, allowances, and food stamps. However, these resources are typically small and cover only basic needs. Research indicates that the young and the old are the two largest age groups currently experiencing unemployment.

ISSUE 06 UNEMPLOYMENT

Vocabulary & Expressions:

harmonized
*to bring into agreement; to make adjustments so that statistics are comparable
- The World Customs Organization maintains a *harmonized* system of standard names and numbers for traded products.

outdated
*no longer in use, out-of-date, outmoded, antiquated
- The last unemployment statistics that we have for East Timor are from 2006, so they are obviously *outdated*.

persistent
*lasting or enduring strongly
- The company's old computer system experienced *persistent* failures.

erode
*to destroy slowly
- Inflation *erodes* the value of our money.

dislocation
*a situation where people or things are out of place
- The war in Syria has led to the *dislocation* of millions of people.

eviction
*a legal process by which someone is expelled or removed from a home for nonpayment of rent or mortgage
- After the renters did not pay their rent for three months, the owner served them with an *eviction* notice.

tent city
*an area set up with tents, especially to house homeless or displaced people
- In 2016, the City of Dallas struggled with how to deal with a *tent city* that housed about 800 homeless people.

susceptibility
*likely to be affected with a disease, infection, or condition
- Most people have more *susceptibility* to colds during the wintertime.

sunny disposition
*an emotional outlook or mood that is generally positive and cheerful
- Optimists are people who have a *sunny disposition*.

look on the bright side
*to concentrate on the positive aspects of a situation, despite the difficulties
- My best friend is a very cheerful person; she always *looks on the bright side* of life.

conscientious
*always acting according to one's conscience or one's inner sense of what is right; always acting in an honest and faithful manner
- Mr. White was a very *conscientious* worker; he worked very hard even when his supervisor was not watching.

allowance
*a sum of money given for a particular purpose, as for expenses
- The company gave the employee an *allowance* of $200 for the business trip.

food stamps
*coupons provided by the U.S. government directly to the poorest citizens, which they can spend like cash for food items
- *Food stamps* can only be used to buy food items; they cannot be used to buy alcohol, tobacco, and other non-food items.

Let's Talk Business

Discussion Points:

1. Do you know any recent college graduates who are having difficulty finding a job? What do they say about their life?
2. What is the current unemployment rate in your country? Do you think it is accurate?
3. What sort of benefits does your country offer people who become unemployed? Do you think your government should do more?
4. Are there any tent cities or other places where homeless people gather in your city? Has the government ever tried to remove the homeless groups?
5. How can a country like Qatar have such a low unemployment rate of only 0.4%?
6. Have you or a member of your family ever experienced unemployment? How would you describe the experience?
7. Do you think that the unemployed in your country are more likely to commit crimes than other people?

Current Hot Topic: The President and Unemployment

Many citizens vote for political candidates because of their promises to increase jobs and reduce unemployment. Statistics show that, when the economy is doing well near an election, the ruling party does well; conversely, when the economy is doing poorly near an election, voters tend to choose the opposition party. However, it is important to ask: how much influence does the president actually have over the economy? Most economists say that presidents get too much praise when the economy does well and too much blame when it declines. In capitalist economies, national economic forces go through cycles, and it's mostly luck that determines how well the economy is doing when it's time for the national election. Most of the changes that a president can make are very subtle and may take months or years to affect the economy.

For Further Discussion:

1. Do you agree with the idea that the president's policies have little effect on the economy? Do you think that principle is true in your country?
2. When it's time to elect a new president in your country, what political topics are most important to you? Is the unemployment rate one of them?

- Why don't you buy this car? I think it's the best car considering price, fuel-efficiency, and maintenance.
- No way! For me, nothing is more important than brand name. This is my favorite!
- Oh, Honey, brand name is nothing but the name itself. It doesn't guarantee anything more than that. I'm sure you'll regret your decision.
- Don't worry. I will love it forever like I love you. Period!

Topic Preview:

What are the most famous brand names in your country? How did those companies create such great reputations? What actions or events can damage a company's brand? If a company's brand name is damaged, is it possible for the company to recover its good reputation?

Dialogue:

Abigail: James, what are the most famous brand names in Canada?

James: Well, one of the most famous would be Cirque du Soleil.

Abigail: Oh, the famous circus? I thought they were from France.

James: Not at all. They are from Montreal in Quebec.

Abigail: I see. What are some other famous Canadian brands?

James: I would certainly include Tim Hortons, which is a famous coffee shop chain.

Abigail: Oh, I've heard of it. Any others you can think of?

James: Of course, there's also Molson Brewery, the Royal Bank of Canada, and IMAX.

Abigail: IMAX is Canadian?

James: Absolutely! The technology was developed in Canada in the late 1960s and early 1970s.

Abigail: Wow, thanks! You've given me a mini-education in Canadian brands!

James: My pleasure!

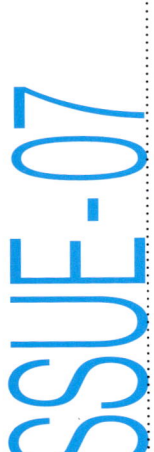

Brand Power

A brand is a name, term, design, or symbol that distinguishes a company or product from its competitors. The process of creating brands is known as "branding." It involves marketing and communication methods that create a favorable and lasting impression in the minds of customers. Branding involves the creation of the following elements related to a specific brand: brand identity, brand communication (using logos and trademarks), brand awareness, brand loyalty, and brand management.

An important step in creating a brand is to choose a memorable name. Brand names may be made from alliterations (Dunkin' Donuts), descriptive expressions (Whole Foods), initials (UPS, IBM), mythical persons (Nike), neologisms (Häagen-Dazs), personal names (Disney), physical landmarks (Fuji Film), puns ("Lord of the Fries"), rhymes (Reece's Pieces), and combinations of words (Microsoft). Regardless of which method is chosen for creating a brand name, the intention is always to come up with a memorable name that customers will regard positively.

Once a brand has become established, it possesses what experts call "brand equity," which is the measure of a brand's total worth. When a product has a high level of brand equity, customers are even willing to pay a higher price for the product because they trust the company and the product. Some brands develop such a lofty level of brand equity that their name becomes a brandnomer. Thus, Xerox is used to mean "photocopy" and Kleenex to mean "facial tissue." If companies are not careful about protecting their brands, they can actually lose their trademark protection. The words *aspirin*, *escalator*, *laundromat*, *thermos*, and *zipper* were all once protected trademarks, but now they are used as generic terms.

Branding is not limited to products and services. Even NGOs and non-profit organizations have brands, such as Amnesty International and World Wildlife Fund. Individuals in business, politics, or entertainment also represent brands, such as Donald Trump, Tom Cruise, and Bill Gates. Sometimes, an individual brand can be damaged beyond repair. Racing cyclist Lance Armstrong represented a valued international brand until he admitted that he had taken performance-enhancing drugs. His brand is unlikely ever to recover.

ISSUE 07 BRAND POWER

Vocabulary & Expressions:

logo
*a graphic representation or symbol of a company name or trademark; also called a *logotype*
- The Nike logo, which is called the Swoosh, is one of the most recognizable brand *logos* in the world.

trademark
*a distinctive name, symbol, figure, letter, word, or mark used exclusively by a company to distinguish its specific products from competing products
- The most famous *trademark* is the world is Apple, the company that was started by Steve Jobs.

alliteration
*the use of two or more words in a word group, all beginning with the same letter or sound
- "Gentle giant," "financial future," and "smooth sailing" are all examples of *alliterations*.

neologism
*a new word or phrase
- One of the most famous *neologisms* of recent years is the word Brexit, which was first used in 2012 to refer to the British exit from the European Union.

pun
*the humorous use of a word or phrase to suggest a different meaning or application; also called a "play on words"
- Here is my favorite *pun*: "I'm on a *seafood* diet; every time I *see food*, I eat it."

rhyme
*words that are similar in sound, especially at the end of lines in a poem
- One good illustration of *rhymes* is found in a poem by Robert Frost:
  The woods are lovely, dark, and *deep*,
  But I have promises to *keep*,
  And miles to go before I *sleep*.

come up with
*to produce, create, supply
- The student could not *come up with* the right answer to the teacher's question.

equity
*the monetary value of a property, business, or other thing
- The brand *equity* of Google is valued at $102 billion.

brandnomer
*a popular trademark that became a general term for all similar products, thus losing its trademark protection
- The word "escalator" is now a *brandnomer*, though originally it was a trademark of the Otis Elevator Company.

generic
*a general word or phrase that is not protected by trademark registration
- The words *salt*, *ramen*, and *cola* are all *generic* terms that cannot be trademarked.

NGO
*abbreviation for a nongovernmental organization
- The World Wildlife Fund (WWF) helps protect nature and is one of the most well-known *NGOs* in the world.

non-profit
*an organization not established for the purpose of making a profit
- The Salvation Army is one of the most famous *non-profit* organizations in the world.

Let's Talk Business

Let's Talk Business

Discussion Points:

1. What are the most famous brand names in your country? Do you own any products with those brand names?
2. Can you think of any examples where a company's brand was harmed by introducing a low-quality product or by some type of scandal?
3. Can you think of any brands that used to be popular but are no longer popular today? What happened to those brands?
4. People can also have a brand. Which person has the best brand recognition in the following fields in your country: business, politics, and entertainment?
5. What are your favorite brands from your country? What are your favorite international brands? Which brand would you prefer for the following products: television, smart phone, car, airline, cinema, shopping mall, hamburger, and soft drink?
6. What are some brands that you dislike and would never use again? Why do you dislike those brands?
7. If you could create a new product, what would you choose for a brand name?

Current Hot Topic: The Olympics and the National Brand

A country can have a brand identity, just like a product. Because South Korea successfully hosted the 1988 Summer Olympics and co-hosted the 2002 World Cup, Korea's brand was enhanced. People around the world saw Korea as a developed country, capable of hosting important international events. However, nowadays, many countries are no longer interested in hosting the Olympics. The 2016 Summer Olympics cost Brazil $20 billion, but the country only received $4.5 billion in benefits. Hungary was considered as a host for the 2024 Olympics, but Hungarian citizens protested against the idea, and Paris was chosen as the host city.

For Further Discussion:

1. Do you think there is real brand enhancement for countries that host international events, or are such events just a waste of money?
2. What international events has your country hosted recently? What events will it host in the future? Do you think that hosting these events will enhance your country's brand identity?

– I'm going shopping. Do you want to join me?
– No, sorry. I always do my shopping online. I can buy anything with my mobile phone. It saves me a lot of time and diligence. Furthermore, most of the items are cheaper in an online market.
– Don't you miss the joy of shopping? I can't feel happy when I buy something online.
– The joy of shopping? You must be kidding! For me, shopping is just a boring and tedious job. Online shopping is a blessing to me.

Topic Preview:

Where do you do most of your shopping: online or offline? What are the advantages and disadvantages of each type of shopping? What types of products are easy to buy online? What types of products would you never buy online? Will online shopping eventually destroy traditional stores?

Dialogue:

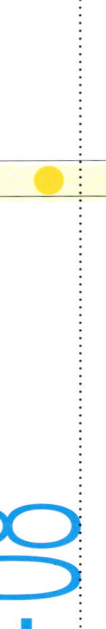

Ben: Harper, is that a new laptop?

Harper: Yes, it is. It's a Samsung Notebook 9 Pro.

Ben: That's the 15-inch model, isn't it?

Harper: Yes, it is. It has the FHD Touch feature, with an Intel Core i7-7500U CPU.

Ben: Wow! That sounds powerful.

Harper: It also has 16gb of RAM and a 256gb SSD.

Ben: That sounds great. By the way, where did you buy it, if I may ask?

Harper: I bought it online at Amazon.

Ben: Was that cheaper than shopping at a regular store?

Harper: I think so, but I bought it mainly for the convenience of shopping online.

Ben: I see. Well, you are truly a high-tech person!

Harper: Thanks!

Internet Shopping

It is unclear when the first commercial transaction was made on the Internet. Pizza Hut started selling pizzas online in August 1994, so they often get credit for making the first online transaction. However, an enterprise called "The Internet Shopping Network," a company that sold computer equipment, debuted online in early 1994. Regardless of who was the first online seller, it is clear that online commerce is big business now. In 2012, online commerce sales topped $1 trillion for the first time in history.

Citizens of almost every country in the world are involved in e-commerce. It appears that the U.K. has the highest per capita online spending. In the Czech Republic, e-commerce represents about one-fourth of the country's entire commercial transactions. China has almost 700 million Internet users, so its e-commerce presence continues to set new records every year. In the first half of 2015, China's online sales reached $253 billion, which was about 10% of the total retail sales in that period. Online sales in China are heavily dominated by Alibaba, which has an e-commerce market share of 80%. China can easily boast that its e-commerce market is the largest in the world. Despite India's massive population, the penetration of Internet sales is low compared to other countries. However, India's e-commerce transactions are growing at a very fast pace.

While Internet commerce sites have provided cheaper goods and more convenience to consumers, they have dealt a heavy blow to traditional brick-and-mortar stores. It is estimated that 15% of America's 1,300 shopping malls will close in the next few years because more people are simply shopping online. In the U.S., once-proud retailers such as Sears and J. C. Penney have experienced sinking sales and profits, forcing them to close hundreds of stores in a desperate attempt to cut their losses. The electronics giant Best Buy experienced a huge slowdown in sales during the 2010s. Many customers would view products at Best Buy but then buy the products online at Amazon. Some experts began to refer jokingly to Best Buy as "Amazon's showroom."

ISSUE 08 INTERNET SHOPPING

Vocabulary & Expressions:

get credit for   *to receive praise or acknowledgment for some accomplishment
- The new CEO *got credit for* the company's increase in sales.

debut   *to appear for the first time
- The world's first rollercoaster *debuted* in Paris in 1817.

per capita   *by or for each individual person
- Americans consumed 11.6 pounds of apples *per capita* in 2014.

set new records   *to establish higher rates or amounts
- Every time the Olympics are held, athletes *set new records* in almost every sport.

market share   *the specific percentage of total sales of a product achieved by a company during a certain period
- Samsung and Apple are losing their smartphone *market share* as Chinese brands continue to grow in popularity.

boast   *to speak with pride about something
- South Korea can *boast* of having the world's fastest Internet speed.

deal a heavy blow   *cause significant damage to something
- The use of email has *dealt a heavy blow* to the profits of the post office.

brick-and-mortar   *pertaining to traditional stores and businesses that have physical buildings and facilities
- Many people now read books on a tablet computer, but others still like to buy books at *brick-and-mortar* bookstores.

once-proud   *previously successful, prominent, and praiseworthy
- The *once-proud* hotel was torn down to make way for a new apartment complex.

cut one's losses   *To remove oneself from a continuously losing situation.
- Joe kept losing money in the stock market, so he sold all his stock to *cut his losses*.

slowdown   *a slowing down or delay in progress, action, profits; a downturn
- Due to the economic *slowdown*, the company decided not to hire any new employees for one year.

showroom   *a room used for the display of goods or merchandise
- IKEA has one of the largest furniture *showrooms* in the city.

Let's Talk Business

Discussion Points:

1. What are the most successful online retailers in your country? How often do you buy from them?
2. What kinds of stores have lost business in your country because of e-commerce?
3. What are some products that you always buy online? What are some products that you would never buy online?
4. Are you concerned about the dangers of online commerce? (e.g., loss of privacy, stolen credit cards)
5. Are shopping malls popular in your country? Do you think that they have lost business because of Internet commerce? Do you know of any shopping malls that have closed?
6. What is your opinion of matchmaking websites? Do you think that they are a legitimate form of e-commerce? How successful do you think they are?
7. Who uses online commerce more, you or your parents? Do you know anyone who refuses to buy things online?

Current Hot Topic: Dominance of Amazon

Founded in 1994, Amazon.com is the largest Internet company by revenue in the world. The company started out as an online bookstore but later diversified to sell DVDs, CDs, software, video games, electronics, clothing, furniture, toys, jewelry, and even food. In 2017, Amazon announced plans to acquire Whole Foods Market for $13.4 billion, which would dramatically increase Amazon's presence in the grocery market. However, the increasing dominance of Amazon in the retail world has many people worried. Some people even accuse Amazon of "bullying tactics" for the manner in which they pressure publishers and producers of various products to reduce their prices. Also, even though Amazon intends to hire thousands of new workers, each new employee at Amazon means that a job in a local community is probably lost forever. Amazon certainly has cheaper prices, but is it ultimately a blessing or a curse?

For Further Discussion:

1. Do you think that Amazon is ultimately good for society? In other words, is it a good result that Amazon now dominates the world of online retailing?
2. Have you ever bought any items from Amazon? Were you happy with your purchases?

— Wow! These candies are magical. According to the ad, the candies lower your blood pressure, prevent strokes, and even strengthen your heart.
— You idiot! Do you really believe such claims?
— Why not?
— Don't you know advertisers will do anything to sell a product, including lying?
— I don't think so. At least, the candies will have a PLACEBO EFFECT.

Topic Preview:

How accurate is the advertising that you see on a daily basis? Do you think that advertising should always be 100% truthful, or is it acceptable to exaggerate a little? If you owned a company, would you always advertise your products with total honesty? Do you think the amount of advertising in today's society is too much, too little, or just the right amount?

Dialogue:

David: Ella, I am so sick of all these TV ads!

Ella: Well, I think most people feel the same way.

David: The TV guide says that the national news show runs from 6:30 to 7:00 pm. That should be 30 minutes of news, right?

Ella: Of course, that's a 30-minute period, but you know there will be some commercials.

David: But out of 30 minutes, how many minutes do you think are devoted to commercials?

Ella: Hmmm...I don't know—maybe six or seven minutes?

David: No, there's a full 10 minutes lost to TV commercials! The 30-minute news program is actually only 20 minutes of news.

Ella: Wow! That's one-third of the program devoted to commercials.

David: Yeah, it's absolutely ridiculous!

Ella: Well, I think you should just buy a DVR. You can record the programs you like, watch them later, and fast forward through the commercials.

David: I think I'll do that, as soon as I save up enough money for the DVR.

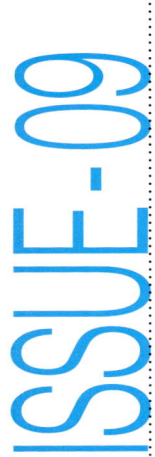

Advertising

Advertising consists of the promotion of goods or services for sale. The advertising may be conducted through traditional impersonal media, such as radio, television, newspapers, magazines, billboards, or through new forms of media, such as blogs, websites, or text messages. Advertisements are usually referred to as "ads" in American English and "adverts" in British English. We usually think of advertisements as designed to promote a consumer product or service. However, many non-commercial advertisers exist, including political parties, religious organizations, special interest groups, and governmental agencies.

In 2015, advertisers spent the staggering figure of $525 billion on advertising. The distribution of advertising among the various media is projected for 2017 as follows: 34.8% on TV, 18.2% on online sites, 18.4% on mobile devices, 10.1% on newspapers, 5.3% on magazines, 6.6% on outdoor signs, 5.9% on radio, and 0.7% in the cinema. Television advertising is the most expensive form of advertising, and the most prominent advertising event on television is the American Super Bowl. More than 108 million viewers watch advertisements that cost $8 million per minute.

Advertisers have been subject to immense criticism for their practices. Critics claim that modern advertising represents a hyper-commercialization of the culture. Others assert that much of advertising is simply "visual pollution." However, advertisements that seem like pollution to some observers are viewed by others as a vibrant part of a city's fabric. Tourists from around the world come to Times Square in New York City to see its huge digital billboards. Likewise, tourists enjoy coming to Central Tokyo to see the commercial panorama of the Ginza. Nevertheless, some cities, including Moscow, are fed up with extensive advertising and have begun a crackdown against over-the-top advertising. In the U.S., several states have banned billboards altogether. São Paulo, Brazil and Grenoble, France have taken similar steps.

Advertisers have also been accused of promoting sexism. Women are often depicted in ads as subservient to men and as a sexual or emotional playtoy. The women are usually shown as ultra thin and are typecast as experts in fashion, cosmetics, and food.

ISSUE 09 ADVERTISING

Vocabulary & Expressions:

media
*the channels of general communication, information, and entertainment in society, including television, radio, newspapers, and magazines
Note: the word *media* is the plural of *medium* and normally takes a plural verb. However, some English speakers use a singular verb.
- The *media* are [is] covering the president's speech tonight.

staggering
*astounding, overwhelming, shocking
- The cost of creating new medicinal drugs is *staggering*.

subject to
*open, exposed, vulnerable
- The politician's broken promises made him *subject to* extensive criticism.

hyper-commercialization
*excessive treatment of things as products to be bought and sold
- Many musicians complain about the current *hyper-commercialization* of the music industry.

vibrant
*moving with vigor and energy
- Many people are leaving rural areas because they enjoy the *vibrant* life of a large city.

fabric
*framework, structure
- Respect for the elderly is part of the *fabric* of Asian society.

billboard
*a flat surface or electronic panel, usually outdoors, on which large advertisements are posted
- The Hilton Hotel has just placed a huge *billboard* in the city center.

panorama
*an extended unbroken view in all directions
- The photographer won an award for his photo featuring a *panorama* of the Grand Canyon at sunset.

crackdown
*the severe or strict enforcement of laws in order to eliminate abuses of the law or to correct a problem
- The city has begun a *crackdown* against illegal taxis.

over-the-top
*beyond normal limits; outrageous, extreme, excessive
- The parents complained that their daughter's new hairstyle was *over-the-top*.

sexism
*attitudes or behavior based on traditional stereotypes of gender roles
- Because the man asked his female co-worker to make coffee, he was accused of *sexism*.

subservient to
*serving or acting in a subordinate or inferior capacity
- In many ancient cultures, women were totally *subservient to* men.

playtoy
*a plaything; someone treated as an object and not as a person
- The young woman broke up with her boyfriend because she felt that he treated her like a *playtoy*.

typecast
*to stereotype
- In the past, men were frequently *typecast* as tough and aggressive and women as meek and submissive.

Let's Talk Business

Discussion Points:

1. Why would any company spend $8 million for a one-minute ad on the Super Bowl?
2. Do you agree with the criticism that much of advertising is simply "visual pollution"?
3. Do you think your city should restrict or even ban billboards? Why or why not?
4. Do you think that ads in your country present stereotypes of men and women?

Read the following quotes about advertising.
Can you explain what they mean? Do you agree with the idea expressed?

5. Advertising is legalized lying. H. G. Wells
6. Nowadays, ads don't just sell a product. They sell an attitude! Bill Watterson
7. The future of advertising is the Internet. Bill Gates

Current Hot Topic: Advertising to Children

The advertising of products to children has been a topic of controversy for some time. Fast-food restaurant chains have been especially criticized for targeting children in their advertisements. Critics claim that fast food is low in nutritional value, and these restaurants should not focus their ads on young children. Canada is a good example of a country that has begun to solve the problem of advertising food to children. Sixteen of the largest food and beverage companies in Canada decided together that they would ensure that at least 50% of their advertisements targeted at children would contain healthier food choices.

For Further Discussion:

1. In a democratic society, shouldn't restaurant chains be able to advertise their products as they see fit? Isn't it the parents' responsibility to monitor their children's eating habits?
2. Would you support more governmental restrictions that would reduce advertising to children in your country?

Poor: You have a moral responsibility to help the poor.
Rich: Why?
Poor: You're getting richer while we're getting poorer. We can't help it.
Rich: Your laziness is the problem! If you work hard, you can make lots of money and live like us.
Poor: You're lying! Don't you see I work from sunrise to sunset every day on the street begging for pennies?

They obviously have very different views of what work is.

Topic Preview:

How rich are the richest people in your country? How much of the wealth in your country do they possess? Is your country's situation like that of the U.S., where the richest 0.1% owns as much wealth as the bottom 90%? What do you think should be done about the problem of wealth inequality?

Dialogue:

Oliver: Grace, I saw a Bernie Sanders sticker on your book bag. Did you vote for Bernie Sanders in the 2016 presidential race?

Grace: Yes, I did! I voted for him to be the Democratic nominee, but of course, he lost to Hillary Clinton. I voted for Clinton in the presidential race, but she lost as well.

Oliver: Why did you support Bernie Sanders, if I may ask?

Grace: I liked his approach to taxation and wealth inequality.

Oliver: What do you mean by "wealth inequality"?

Grace: Well, as Sanders pointed out often, "The top one-tenth of one percent owns almost as much wealth as the bottom 90 percent."

Oliver: That's shocking!

Grace: Yes, it is. The huge concentration of wealth means that the U.S. has the highest childhood poverty rate of any developed country on earth.

Oliver: Unbelievable! Well, what was Sanders' solution to this problem?

Grace: He said that we have to demand that the wealthy corporations pay their fair share in taxes. Also, they cannot shift their profits and jobs overseas to avoid paying taxes.

Oliver: Well, that all sounds reasonable to me. I hope he becomes president during the next election.

Wealth Inequality

The term "wealth inequality" refers to the unequal distribution of assets among the citizens of a country. This phenomenon is also referred to as "economic inequality," "income inequality," or "the wealth gap." Economists who study this issue usually focus on economic disparity in three metrics: wealth, income, and consumption. The issue of wealth inequality is sometimes viewed from a global perspective. For example, in 2017, an Oxfam study concluded that eight rich people, six of whom were Americans, owned as much wealth as "half the human race."

Besides the global perspective, wealth inequality can also be viewed from a national perspective. In 2015, the OECD published a research report entitled *In It Together: Why Less Inequality Benefits All*. The study concluded that that greater wealth inequality hinders long-term economic growth. Indeed, the OECD estimates that the increasing wealth gap over the past two decades has reduced economic growth among its 35 member nations by almost five percentage points. While globalization has reduced wealth inequality among nations, it has increased wealth inequality within nations.

The issue of wealth inequality took center stage in the 2016 U.S. presidential race. Senator Bernard Sanders, who challenged Hillary Clinton in the race to become the Democratic nominee for president was fond of saying, "Today, we live in the richest country in the history of the world, but that reality means little because much of that wealth is controlled by a tiny handful of individuals. The issue of wealth and income inequality is the great moral issue of our time, it is the great economic issue of our time, and it is the great political issue of our time." Part of Sanders's solution was to increase taxes on the rich and to raise the minimum wage to $15 per hour. Because Sanders was gaining support, Clinton had no choice but to go along with many of Sanders's proposals. The wealth inequality in the U.S. is also connected to racial wealth inequality. Studies have shown that white Americans have 13 times as much wealth as black Americans and 10 times as much wealth as Hispanic Americans.

ISSUE 10 WEALTH INEQUALITY

Vocabulary & Expressions:

disparity *lack of similarity or equality; inequality, difference; often used in expressions such as disparity in age, disparity in rank, disparity in wealth
- When an 89-year-old man married a 26-year-old woman, many people were shocked by the age *disparity*.

metrics *a standard for measuring or evaluating something, especially one that uses figures or statistics; also used as a suffix, *-metrics*, to refer to the application of statistics and mathematical analysis to a field of study (e.g., *biometrics*, *econometrics*)
- By any *metrics*, Taylor Swift's recent concert tour was an amazing success.

Oxfam *an international group of charitable organizations focused on reducing global poverty; founded in 1942 in Oxford, England
- The motto of *Oxfam* shows clearly its main purpose: "the power of people against poverty."

OECD *abbreviation for The Organisation for Economic Co-operation and Development, an international economic organization with 36 member countries, founded in 1960 to promote economic progress and world trade.
  Note: The official name of the organization uses the British spelling *organisation*.
- The newest member of the *OECD* is Lithuania, which joined on July 5, 2018.

hinder *to cause delay; to interrupt, hamper, impede
- The recent hurricane *hindered* the state's economic progress.

take center stage *to be in a position of maximum importance, visibility, or prominence
- During the Olympics, the world's greatest athletes *take center stage* on TV sports programs.

nominee *a person chosen, or nominated, to run for elective office
- There were two main *nominees* in the 2016 U.S. presidential race: Hillary Clinton for the Democrats and Donald Trump for the Republicans.

be fond of *to have a liking or affection for
- My mother *was* always *fond of* saying, "Better late than never."

go along with *to accept or comply with some proposal; to acquiesce
- The employees had no choice but to *go along with* the supervisor's foolish plan.

racial wealth inequality *an economic situation where a gap exists in money and possessions between different races of people
- The average black family in the U.S. holds about 15.7% of the wealth that the average white family holds, a fact that shows the wide *racial wealth inequality* in the U.S.

black Americans *an ethnic group of Americans with total or partial ancestry from any of the black racial groups of Africa; synonymous with *African Americans* (spelled *African-American* when used as an adjective)
- *Black Americans* represent about 12.7% of the U.S. population.

Hispanic Americans *a person of Latin-American or Spanish descent living in the U.S.; synonymous with *Latino Americans*
- *Hispanic Americans* represent about 17.8% of the U.S. population.

Let's Talk Business

Discussion Points:

1. Do you think that wealth inequality is a natural result of living in a democratic country, where people have the freedom to work hard and get richer?
2. Should governments place higher taxes on the rich in order to reduce wealth inequality? If you were rich, would you be willing to pay higher taxes?
3. How great is the wealth inequality in your country? Do politicians ever talk about the issue?
4. Would you rather live in a country with high wealth inequality or low wealth inequality?
5. Do rich countries have a moral obligation to help poor countries financially? What sort of help should rich countries provide?
6. Has your country ever offered financial help to a poorer country? What sort of help did your country give?
7. Is there any racial wealth inequality in your country? Is there wealth inequality between citizens and foreign workers?

Current Hot Topic: Reducing Wealth Inequality by Taxing the Rich

Most people agree that wealth inequality is undesirable from both an economic and social perspective. However, what is the best way to reduce wealth inequality? Many politicians and economists believe that putting higher taxes on the rich is the fastest and most equitable way to achieve that goal. There is some evidence to support this idea. In 2013, President Barack Obama and the U.S. Congress negotiated an increase in taxes on the richest Americans. The new taxes represented the first significant change in taxes on the wealthy in 20 years. Data showed that the new taxes resulted in an abrupt decline in income inequality.

For Further Discussion:

1. Do you think that the problem of wealth inequality can be solved by increasing taxes on the rich? Why or why not?
2. In the U.S., the Democratic Party usually supports higher taxes on the rich, and the pro-business Republican Party opposes higher taxes. Do you have a similar situation with political parties in your country?

I want to buy a house in a couple of years. So we have to save diligently.

We don't have to buy a house. Instead, we can rent an apartment FOREVER!

I don't care if they buy a house or not. I just want more snacks!

I don't care about snacks. I just want them to walk me more often!

Topic Preview:

Which is wiser, to buy a house or rent a house? Which is better, to buy a car or rent a car? When can renting be better than buying something and owning it? How large is the rental market in your country?

Dialogue:

Victoria: Jayden, I hear you're thinking about buying a house.

Jayden: Yes, that's right. My wife and I are thinking seriously about it. What about you? Do you own or rent?

Victoria: Well, my husband and I decided just to rent a house for a few years.

Jayden: Oh? What was the deciding factor for you?

Victoria: Well, we aren't sure that we are going to stay in this area. We'd eventually like to move closer to where my parents live, which is 500 miles from here.

Jayden: I see. So how long have you been renting?

Victoria: Well, it's been two years now. So far, we've been happy with our decision.

Jayden: I see. My case is a little different, I think, because we want to live here permanently.

Victoria: In that case, it may be better to buy a house.

Jayden: Yeah, maybe. It's a big decision. To buy or to rent: that is the question.

To Buy or To Rent?

There are many reasons why people would choose to rent instead of buy. For example, in many countries, rent used for business purposes is tax-deductible, but rent on a dwelling is not tax-deductible. Another reason for renting something is obvious: people don't have enough money to buy the item that is needed. They have no other choice but to rent. Also, if people only need something temporarily, they will likely rent it, such as a car or bicycle.

Many young couples deliberate extensively on the issue of buying or renting a house. Some experts even claim that the decision to buy a home is more of an emotional decision than a financial one. People who aspire to homeownership are often motivated by the desire to control their living space, to have more privacy, and to establish a place to raise their family. Unfortunately, the home that you bought can change abruptly from an asset to a liability. If someone bought a house in the U.S. in 2006, they saw the value of their house decline quickly, and they were under water until 2013, when prices began to rise again.

The rental market is expanding not only with respect to houses but also in other areas. The global car rental market was valued at $58 billion in 2016 and is expected to reach $125 billion by 2022. Besides cars, people rent many other types of items, including ships, aircraft, specialized tools, large equipment, furniture, designer handbags, and electrical items.

The concept of renting has led to a business model known as the access economy or on-demand economy. The best examples of this model are Airbnb and Uber. Airbnb is a hospitality service that enables people to lease or rent short-term lodging, which is often in their own home. Airbnb now boasts over 3,000,000 listings in 65,000 cities and 191 countries. Uber is a car transportation system for people and a food delivery service. However, both Airbnb and Uber have met with numerous legal challenges and restrictions in cities where they operate.

ISSUE 11 TO BUY OR TO RENT?

Vocabulary & Expressions:

tax-deductible *an expense, loss, or charitable contribution that can be subtracted from the total amount on which tax is calculated
- The government encourages people to donate money to charities by making those donations *tax-deductible*.

deliberate *to think carefully or attentively; to reflect on a matter
- The woman *deliberated* for a long time before giving her decision about the man's marriage proposal.

aspire to *to desire strongly, to seek ambitiously, especially for something of great value
- Because her father was a famous physician, the young woman also *aspired to* become a physician.

liability *money owed; a financial obligation; opposite of *asset*
- Expenses are the costs of a company's operation, but *liabilities* are the debts that the company owes.

under water *holding an asset that is worth less than its purchase price or the debt owed on it
- When the housing bubble burst, many homeowners were *under water* because they owed more money on their house than it was worth.

specialized tool *a piece of equipment, usually handheld, that is used to perform or facilitate mechanical operations
- A chainsaw is a *specialized tool* used for cutting down trees.

designer handbag *a woman's small bag, carried to contain personal articles, which is labeled with a famous designer's name
- After winning the lottery, the man bought his wife an expensive *designer handbag* made by Louis Vuitton.

electrical item *a device that is operated by electrical power; to be distinguished from an *electronic item*, which also uses electrical power but which modifies it through the use of semiconductors that perform electron control for creative purposes such as processing, transmitting, or outputting information
- A toaster is an *electrical item*, but a television is an *electronic* item.

access economy *a business model where goods and services are offered on the basis of access rather than ownership
- With Airbnb, consumers participate in the *access economy* by booking a room through their smart phone.

on-demand economy *a business model where goods and services are offered immediately when they are requested
- Netflix is part of the *on-demand economy* because members have immediate access to thousands of movies and TV shows to watch whenever they choose.

hospitality service *the act of providing a homestay (accommodation in a home) for travelers, either for pay or for free
- Both Airbnb and Couchsurfing offer *hospitality services*, but Airbnb requires a payment, while Couchsurfing is free.

meet with *to encounter or experience
- The president's proposal for higher taxes was *met with* immediate opposition by Congress.

Let's Talk Business

Let's Talk Business

Discussion Points:

1. Do young couples in your country usually buy a house or rent one? If they buy, where do they get such a large sum of money?
2. Is it expensive to rent a 2-bedroom apartment in your country? What about an office space?
3. Considering the economic situation today, would you prefer to buy a house or rent one?
4. Some people claim that home prices will always increase in value, so it's always a good choice to buy a house. Do you agree with that idea?
5. When you get married, which would you prefer: to live with your parents or to buy your own home?
6. Have you ever participated in the access economy? What aspect did you participate in? Were you satisfied with the product or service?
7. What are some items that you have rented often? What is something that you would never rent?

Current Hot Topic: Government Control of the Access Economy

The idea of an access economy where individual consumers can benefit from immediate access to products and services sounds like a great idea. However, in actual practice, companies that are involved in the access economy have faced serious opposition by local governments. In the State of New York, hosts cannot rent their home for less than 30 consecutive days unless they are currently living in the property. In Berlin, legislators have prohibited hosts from renting their property on a short-term basis without first getting permission from local authorities. Also, hosts cannot rent more than 50% of their property space. In April 2017, a court in Seoul fined ride service provider Uber a total of $9,000 for running an illegal taxi business that was in violation of the Passenger Transport Service Act.

For Further Discussion:

1. Should governments enact strict regulations for companies participating in the access economy, or should those companies be allowed to develop according to market forces?
2. To what extent does your local government control providers in the access economy? Do you think the government should exercise more or less control?

As a last resort, earthmen finally started traveling to space. Their mission is to capture the sun and moon and sell them to the ETs to pay off their debt. They think they'll have no problem capturing the moon, but the sun is different because it is still burning. So they have prepared a big fire extinguisher. If their mission is accomplished successfully, all debt problems on Earth will be resolved.

Topic Preview:

What should happen to people who cannot pay their debts? Should they be sent to prison, or is there another option? Should governments be allowed to borrow money just like people? What should happen to a company or government that cannot pay its debts?

Dialogue:

Madison: Elijah, I heard that you are going to graduate from college next month.

Elijah: Yes, that's right. I'm already looking for a job.

Madison: Well, congratulations on your accomplishment and good luck with the job search.

Elijah: Thanks! I need to get a job soon and start paying on my student loans.

Madison: Oh, you have student loans to pay off?

Elijah: Yeah, I had no choice but to finance my college education with student loans.

Madison: I see. How long do you think it will take to pay off that debt?

Elijah: I'm not sure exactly, but it will take years. At least I have a low interest rate.

Madison: Yeah, that's good. Well, if you get a good enough job, you can pay off the loans soon.

Elijah: Thanks for your encouragement. I need it!

Debt

The word "debt" refers to money owed by one party, the debtor or borrower, to another party, the creditor or lender. There are three kinds of borrowers: individuals, businesses, and governments. However, there are many kinds of lenders: individuals, loan sharks, banks, credit card companies, countries, and international financial organizations. When a debt is incurred, lenders always establish some contractual obligations concerning the amount and timing of repayments of principal and interest, as well as any penalties that borrowers may face in case they make a late payment or go into default.

In most cases, debts are represented by written contracts, though in the case of an individual-to-individual loan, a gentleman's agreement may suffice. In the case of large debts, the lender may require the borrower to present collateral as part of the agreement. If someone borrows money to buy a house, they must sign a mortgage. The word "debt" can also be used metaphorically to refer to personal obligations that are not financial. For example, if a person helps someone, the person being helped owes a "debt of gratitude" to the person helping.

When individuals borrow so much money that they cannot repay their loans, they may have no choice but to opt for bankruptcy, a legal status established for people who lack the money to pay off their financial obligations. If the bankruptcy is approved, the borrower's debt is wiped clean. However, the person may not declare bankruptcy again for seven years. Also, some debts cannot be discharged in bankruptcy: taxes owed to the government, child support payments owed by divorced parents, and student loans.

What happens in the case of countries that cannot pay off their debts? Can they also declare bankruptcy? If a country cannot repay its debts, it is said to go into default, which is similar to going bankrupt. However, countries rarely refuse to pay anything at all toward their debts. Instead, they try to restructure their debt, which means that they will offer to repay part of the original debt. In 2001, Argentina suffered an $81 billion default, and they offered to repay their creditors only one-third of what was owed. Creditors who accept such a small repayment are said to "take a haircut."

ISSUE 12 DEBT

Vocabulary & Expressions:

loan shark
*a person who lends money at very high rates of interest, which are sometimes illegal
- The police arrested the **loan shark**, who they found out was working for the Mafia.

incur
*to bring upon oneself some undesirable situation
- American college students often **incur** a lot of debt during their years in college.

contractual
*related to a contract or formal agreement between two parties
- The professor's **contractual** obligation was to teach four courses every semester.

principal
*the original amount of a debt on which interest is calculated
- The student repaid the **principal**, which was $1,000, along with another $200 in interest.

default
*a condition where people cannot pay their financial obligations
- Because Mr. Jones lost his job, he could not repay his debts, and they went into **default**.

gentleman's agreement
*a personal agreement based on honor and not legally binding
- When Mr. Smith borrowed $100 from his friend, the two simply shook hands and Smith made a **gentleman's agreement** to repay the money in one month.

suffice
*to be enough, adequate
- The couple agreed that $1,000 in cash would **suffice** for their vacation to Miami.

collateral
*security pledged for the payment of a loan
- Ms. Johnson used her 5,000 shares of Samsung stock as **collateral** for the money she borrowed.

mortgage
*an agreement in which a person borrows money to buy a house or other type of property, and the lender can take possession of the property if the borrower fails to repay the money
- Mr. and Mrs. Smith didn't have enough money to buy the $300,000 house, so they paid $60,000 and signed a **mortgage** loan for the rest.

metaphorically
*using a figure of speech in which a term or phrase is applied to something in a non-literal manner in order to suggest a resemblance
- When John said the actress was an angel, of course he was speaking **metaphorically**.

opt
*to choose, make a choice (usually followed by *for*)
- Ms. Miller did not drink alcohol, so she **opted** for a cup of tea.

wipe clean
*to erase or remove completely
- Because the student returned the stolen book and apologized, his negative record was **wiped clean**.

discharge
*cancellation of an obligation, especially that of repaying a loan
- Even though Mr. Jackson declared bankruptcy, his taxes could not be **discharged**, so he had still to pay them.

take a haircut
*to take a huge financial loss, especially when a loan or investment is not fully repaid
- The company was a complete failure, so all the investors **took a haircut** when they got back only 10% of their money.

Let's Talk Business

Let's Talk Business

Discussion Points:

1. Has your country ever defaulted on a debt? What happened? Was the debt eventually repaid?
2. When countries cannot repay their debts, they are frequently lent money by the International Monetary Fund (IMF). Is this a good solution or should the world just let the country go into default?
3. How common is personal bankruptcy in your country? Are there any debts that cannot be discharged in bankruptcy?
4. Do you think a personal bankruptcy is a moral failure? Why or why not?
5. Have you ever needed to borrow money? Who did you borrow it from? Did you repay the loan on time?
6. Have you ever made a gentleman's agreement with someone? What did the two of you agree to do? Did both of you fulfill your part of the agreement?
7. Benjamin Franklin said, "Creditors have better memories than debtors." What did he mean?

Current Hot Topic: The Largest Debtor Nation

The term "external debt," when applied to a country, refers to the total public and private debt owed by the country to others outside the country. Based on that definition, the United States of America is the largest debtor nation in the world. The U.S. currently owes more than $20 trillion, which represents more than $60,000 per citizen. It is difficult to see how this money could ever be repaid. The issue of the national debt is brought up in every U.S. presidential election, but in the end, politicians never do anything to slow the ever mounting national debt. There is even a website, usdebtclock.org, where you can watch the national debt clock in real time.

For Further Discussion:

1. If the U.S. has such an astronomical national debt, why do people still accept the U.S. dollar? Will it ever be replaced by a stronger currency?
2. Does your country have a large national debt? Would you be willing to pay more in taxes so that the national debt could be paid off?

- Don't pump the balloon anymore. I'm afraid it'll burst.
- Don't worry. There's still room for more air.
- Stop! Enough is enough! We can make enough money at this size of the balloon!
- No way! The more air we pump into the balloon, the larger profits we can get.

I'm going to burst the balloon right now before people suffer from a disastrous economic bubble.

Topic Preview:

What happens during an economic bubble? Why do people spend wildly on stocks and real estate as though prices will always go up? Who is hurt most when an economic bubble bursts? How can you identify an economic bubble?

Dialogue:

Sofia: Logan, you're from Australia, right?

Logan: That's right. Why do you ask?

Sofia: I've been reading about a possible housing bubble in Australia. Do you think it's real?

Logan: I don't know exactly. Experts have been debating this issue since 2001.

Sofia: But the housing market has not collapsed yet?

Logan: No, prices just keep climbing. No one can predict what will happen.

Sofia: Do you own any property?

Logan: Yes, I do. I own a small condominium that I'm currently renting out.

Sofia: I see. Are you worried about a possible housing bubble?

Logan: Not at all. Fortunately, I paid cash for the condo, so there's no mortgage.

Sofia: Well, it sounds as though you are in good shape.

Economic Bubbles

An economic bubble, or asset bubble, occurs when trade in an asset greatly exceeds the asset's intrinsic value. The asset most often involved in economic bubbles is stocks or real estate, but a bubble could evolve concerning anything of value, including gold and silver. One recent example of an economic bubble occurred in the U.S. housing market during the period of 2006-2012. In the early 2000s, housing prices kept climbing, and many people thought there was no end in sight. If you bought a house for $200,000 in the year 2000, you might have sold it for $300,000 six years later. However, in early 2006, housing prices began to decline and, if you tried to sell the house in 2008 or 2009, you might have gotten less money than what you paid in 2000. Thus, the American real estate market in the early 2000s was a textbook example of an economic bubble. To make matters worse, there was also a recession. Many people lost their jobs and then lost their houses in foreclosure.

To date, economists have not agreed on any specific theory as to why economic bubbles occur. Some have suggested that economic bubbles occur when a country's central bank allows excessive monetary liquidity into the financial system. If there is too much money available, banks may adopt lax lending standards with the result that people borrow more money. If the interest rate is low, people will speculate more with their money, which in turn will cause volatile asset price changes in markets. In other words, economic bubbles occur when there is too much money being spent on too few assets. As a result, both good assets and bad assets appreciate excessively to unsustainable levels.

Identifying economic bubbles in real time is difficult. They are most often identified only in retrospect when asset prices begin to sink. However, indicators of a possible economic bubble include the following: increased use of credit to purchase assets, lending to borrowers with low credit scores, international trade imbalances, and lower interest rates.

ISSUE 13 ECONOMIC BUBBLES

Vocabulary & Expressions:

asset
*a possession of value that could be turned into cash; opposite of *liability*
- If your *assets* are much greater than your liabilities, you are in good financial shape.

intrinsic
*relating to the essential nature of a thing; the inherent, underlying, essential value of something
- The *intrinsic* value of a stock is the value that is supported by the facts and not by speculation.

evolve
*to develop gradually
- Steve Jobs started Apple in his garage, but the company *evolved* into one of the most powerful in the world.

no end in sight
*a situation where one cannot see a limit, boundary, or a final point
- Prices continue to increase with *no end in sight*.

textbook example
*a phenomenon that is so typical and classic that it would be suitable for inclusion in a textbook; also known as *textbook case*
- *Raiders of the Lost Ark* is a *textbook example* of an action-adventure film.

foreclosure
*the taking of someone's property because they fail to make the mortgage payments for it
- During a period of high unemployment, many people lose their homes to *foreclosure*.

liquidity
*a situation where a person, business, or country has significant amounts of cash
- The CEO was pleased with his company's *liquidity* because they had millions of dollars in the bank.

lax
*not strict or severe; careless or negligent
- The teacher was very *lax* about rules in the classroom, so students frequently misbehaved.

volatile
*liable to sudden, unpredictable, or dramatic change
- It is impossible to predict where gold prices will be next year because the price of gold is so *volatile*.

appreciate
*to increase in value
- Many people buy old paintings in hopes that their value will *appreciate* over time.

unsustainable
*not capable of being supported, maintained, or upheld
- Scientists warn against *unsustainable* fishing methods that may lead to the end of seafood.

in retrospect
*looking back on past events; reflecting about the past
- *In retrospect*, I should have studied much harder in college.

Let's Talk Business

Let's Talk Business

Discussion Points:

1. Why is it so difficult for economists to agree on an explanation as to why economic bubbles occur?
2. Has your country experienced an economic bubble during your lifetime? What kind of bubble was it?
3. Do you think there are any markets in your country now that are in danger of becoming a bubble?
4. How easy is it for a person to borrow money to buy a house in your country? Do you think it should be easier or more difficult?
5. Have you ever invested money in something because it was very popular at the time? What happened?

Read the following quotes by Warren Buffett.
Can you explain how these ideas might help you survive a bubble stock market?

6. Be fearful when others are greedy and be greedy when others are fearful.
7. Price is what you pay. Value is what you get.

Current Hot Topic: Government Bailouts When Economic Bubbles Burst

The word "bailout" refers to the situation where the government gives economic support to an important company that faces serious financial problems or bankruptcy. When economic bubbles burst, many banks and companies may face financial ruin. Should the government provide a bailout for the largest ones? Those who say yes claim that some companies are such an important part of the national economy that they are simply "too big to fail." The U.S. Treasury followed this view in 2008-09 when it bailed out numerous large banks, insurance companies, and automobile manufacturers. However, many people argued that the government should not have intervened and should have allowed those companies to fail.

For Further Discussion:

1. Do you think that governments should provide financial support to large banks, insurance companies, and manufacturers that are failing? Why or why not?
2. Are there any companies in your country that are "too big to fail"? What are they?

Apple: You've infringed our patents. You should pay reparations for what you've done to us.
Samsung: What are you talking about? We've never done anything wrong to you! Don't you know we have lots of patents? We don't have to violate anyone's patent.
Apple: We don't think so. We'll see you in court.
Samsung: Do you still want to continue this kind of ridiculous lawsuit? Let's stop right now!
Apple: If we stopped our lawsuits against you, what would you give us in return?
Samsung: What do you want?
Apple: Close your eyes when we use your patents!

Topic Preview:

Have you ever read about a person or company trying to steal another company's invention? What happened? Have you ever had an idea for an invention? What sort of invention would you create? What would you do if someone tried to steal your idea?

Dialogue:

Evelyn: Matthew, do you have any experience with patents?

Matthew: I don't personally, but my uncle has gotten patents for several inventions. Are you planning to invent something?

Evelyn: Well, I have an idea for an invention.

Matthew: That sounds interesting. What sort of invention?

Evelyn: Actually, I'm trying to keep it a secret. I don't want anyone to steal my idea.

Matthew: Well, I promise I won't steal your idea! I'm your friend!

Evelyn: Okay, if you promise. I would like to invent an electronic mosquito killer for indoor use.

Matthew: Hmmm…I'm afraid that's already been invented. I saw one of those on Amazon the other day.

Evelyn: You're kidding!

Matthew: No, I'm not kidding. The company is called Aspectek, and the mosquito killer sells for about $35.

Evelyn: Oh well. I guess I'll have to invent something else.

Patent Wars

A patent is a set of exclusive rights granted by a government to an inventor to manufacture, use, and sell an invention for a certain number of years. To obtain a patent, the inventor must make a public disclosure of details about the invention. Patents are a specific form of intellectual property and must be distinguished from copyrights, trademarks, and trade secrets. The procedure for obtaining a patent and the extent of patent rights vary widely according to international agreements.

If people want to use or sell a patented invention, they must get a license from the patent holder. If they use or sell the invention without a license, they have committed patent infringement. However, cases of infringement are not always clear, so companies often end up filing lawsuits against each other in court. One of the most well-known series of lawsuits concerning patent infringements occurred between Apple and Samsung Electronics, two companies that manufacture more than half of all smart phones sold worldwide. In early 2011, Apple began litigating against Samsung, accusing it of patent infringement. The fierce legal battles between the two companies became known as the "smart phone patent wars."

By July 2012, Apple and Samsung were embroiled in more than 50 lawsuits around the globe, with each company claiming billions of dollars in damages. While Apple gained a legal victory in the U.S., Samsung won rulings in South Korea, Japan, and the U.K. In the U.S., a federal court ruled that Samsung had to pay nearly $400 million to Apple. However, Samsung appealed the decision, and the U.S. Supreme Court reversed the amount of the award. The seven-year patent fight ended in mid-2018 when the parties agreed to an out-of-court financial settlement, though the amount of the settlement was not disclosed. According to law professor Brian J. Love, the lawsuits didn't really accomplish anything. He explained, "Close to a decade of litigation, hundreds of millions of dollars spent on lawyers, and at the end of the day, no products went off the market."

Many patent holders, especially those in the United States, must deal with the problem of frivolous patent lawsuits. These are most often brought by what are known as "patent trolls," individuals who file a patent lawsuit with little or no legal basis. Some companies will pay the patent troll some money just to end the lawsuit.

ISSUE 14 PATENT WARS

Vocabulary & Expressions:

exclusive
*belonging to one individual or group and not to any other; not shared with any other
- MGM had the *exclusive* rights to produce the film *Gone with the Wind*.

disclosure
*making something known; revealing or uncovering
- The politician was shocked by the *disclosure* of details of his private life in the newspaper.

intellectual property
*a legal term referring to property that was created from original artistic thought, such as patents, copyright material, and trademarks
- If you write a song, that song is automatically your *intellectual property*.

trade secret
*a formula, practice, process, design, or collection of information that a company keeps secret from competitors
- The formula for Coca-Cola is a classic example of a *trade secret*.

license
*the legal right to use a patent owned by another
- The university received a *license* from Microsoft to use MS Word on all the university computers.

infringement
*to violate or break a law, agreement, or right of another party
- In 2017, Qualcomm sued Apple for *infringement* of Qualcomm's patent for technology that improves smart phone battery life.

litigate
*to bring a claim in a lawsuit
- It is easier for rich people to *litigate* their complaints because they can hire the best lawyers.

embroiled
*to become involved in trouble, conflict, or argument
- The United Nations was reluctant to get its forces *embroiled* in a civil war.

appeal
*a legal term meaning to ask a higher court to review the decision of a lower court
- The hospital said that they would *appeal* the judge's decision against them.

frivolous
*not serious or reasonable in content, attitude, or behavior; silly
- Some Americans filed a lawsuit claiming that President Obama was not born in the U.S., but a judge dismissed the claim as *frivolous*.

troll
*a person who deliberately posts provocative statements on the Internet just to harass others and make them angry; also used in the expression *patent troll* to refer to someone who files frivolous patent lawsuits
- Internet *trolls* frequently criticize other people's grammar just to make them angry.

Let's Talk Business

Let's Talk Business

Discussion Points:

1. Have you ever read about the lawsuits involving Apple and Samsung Electronics? Who do you think should win that patent war?
2. Have you ever read about any patent wars in your country? What happened?
3. Do you think that patent trolls should be punished? What sort of punishment is suitable?
4. Can you think of any trade secrets, besides the formula for Coca-Cola?
5. Can you think of any other examples of frivolous lawsuits? What happened?
6. Have you ever filed a lawsuit, or thought about filing one? What was your complaint?
7. Has anyone ever threatened to sue you or someone you know? What was their complaint?

Current Hot Topic: The English Rule versus the American Rule

With respect to lawsuits, there are two basic rules that can be followed concerning attorneys' fees. If a legal system follows the English Rule, then the person who loses a lawsuit must pay the other party's attorney's fees. If the American Rule is followed, then each side of the lawsuit is responsible for its own attorney's fees. Almost every Western democracy, except for the U.S., follows the English Rule. There has been discussion about using the English Rule in the U.S., but at present, it is used in only one state, Alaska.

For Further Discussion:

1. Does your country follow the English Rule? Do you think it's more reasonable than the American Rule?
2. Many people claim that the American Rule leads to many frivolous lawsuits. Do you think that claim is true? Why or why not?

Thanks to artificial intelligence, I always have my robot drive me to wherever I want to go. Technical development is always good.

Artificial intelligence has gone too far. Now I work for my robot boss, and he is a backseat driver whenever I drive for him. I yearn for the days when we humans were masters of the robots.

Topic Preview:

Are there any limits to the development of artificial intelligence? Will it be able to drive cars better than human drivers? What sort of jobs will artificial intelligence replace? Will computers someday be smarter than humans?

Dialogue:

Avery: Lucas, did you hear about Amazon's plans for delivering packages in the future?

Lucas: No, I haven't. How are they going to do it?

Avery: They're planning to use drones to deliver packages within 30 minutes after someone places an order.

Lucas: You must be kidding!

Avery: No, I'm not kidding at all. Artificial intelligence can make it happen.

Lucas: I'm very skeptical that they can actually pull this off.

Avery: Well, Jeff Bezos, Amazon's CEO, is a very smart man. I wouldn't count him out.

Lucas: Yes, I know he's smart and rich, but think of all the problems that drones would face.

Avery: Like what?

Lucas: For example, how could they deliver during rain, snow, and other kinds of bad weather?

Avery: Well, they will have to figure that out.

Lucas: I don't think it will ever happen. I'll believe it when I see it.

Artificial Intelligence

Artificial intelligence (AI) is intelligence shown by machines and computers rather than humans or other animals, which have natural intelligence (NI). In computer science, AI is defined as the study and use of "intelligent agents," which are any devices that can understand their environment and take some actions that will cause them to succeed at a goal. Colloquially, AI is defined as a machine that shows cognitive functions that are usually associated with human beings, such as learning and problem solving. AI currently includes the following capabilities: understanding human speech; competing in strategic game systems, such as chess and *go* (known as *baduk* in Korea); operating autonomous cars; routing deliveries; simulating military situations; and interpreting complex data.

The applications of artificial intelligence in modern society are in continuous development. AI is now being used for medical diagnosis, electronic trading on the stock market, and remote sensing. In the field of education, intelligent tutoring systems (ITS) are used widely in the military to teach Air Force technicians how to diagnose problems in the electrical systems of aircraft. With respect to the stock market, AI is used extensively for automated trading systems. One AI system is capable of making millions of stock trades during a day without any human intervention.

In the field of healthcare, artificial intelligence is assisting doctors to find the optimal treatments for various types of cancer. AI is also used for diagnosis. One medical study concluded that AI was as good as trained doctors in identifying skin cancers. In the automotive industry, AI is being used by more than 30 companies to create self-driving vehicles.

Artificial intelligence is already leading to the replacement of human workers in many fields. In 2016, American businessman Andrew Puzder created a stir when he extolled the virtues of using robots instead of human workers in the fast-food industry. He said, "Robots are always polite, they always upsell, they never take a vacation, they never show up late, there's never a slip-and-fall, or an age, sex, or race discrimination case."

ISSUE 15 ARTIFICIAL INTELLIGENCE

Vocabulary & Expressions:

colloquially   *informally; referring to an expression used in ordinary or familiar conversation rather than formal speech
- The Metropolitan Museum of Art in New York City is known *colloquially* as "The Met."

cognitive   *related to the act or process of knowing
- The term "*cognitive* development" refers to the growth of a child's ability to think and reason.

strategic   *requiring a plan, method, or series of actions for obtaining a specific goal or result
- *Strategic* thinking is a process that enhances leaders' practical thinking skills so that they can make the best business decisions.

autonomous   *not subject to control from outside; independent
- An *autonomous* car is also known as a driverless car, self-driving car, or robotic car.

route   *to choose the best course, way, or road for travel
- The U.S. Postal Service has 40,000 zip codes, which it uses to *route* mail delivery in the most efficient way.

simulate   *to create a simulation, likeness, or model of a situation
- Teachers who train nurses often *simulate* a disaster to give students practice in how to respond.

application   *the special use or purpose for which something is used
- Microbiology is an exciting field of study that has many *applications* in medicine.

remote sensing   *the science of gathering information about an object or area from a considerable distance
- Spy satellites use *remote sensing* to detect and classify objects on Earth.

diagnose   *to determine the cause or nature of a disorder, malfunction, or problem by considering the symptoms
- I need a good mechanic to *diagnose* the problems with my car.

optimal   *most favorable or desirable; best; same meaning as *optimum*
- Many snacks have too much sugar and do not offer *optimal* nutrition.

create a stir   *to cause a state of general excitement, commotion, controversy, or shock
- The president's speech *created a stir* because he mentioned the possibility of raising taxes.

extol the virtues of   *to tell people how good something is
- The professor *extolled the virtues* of learning a second language.

upsell   *to try to convince a customer to buy another item or a more expensive item
- Many restaurants train their staff to *upsell* by convincing customers to order more drinks and desserts.

Let's Talk Business

Discussion Points:

1. Do you think that AI will someday exceed human intelligence?
2. What are the best examples of AI that you have seen in your country?
3. Do you think that autonomous cars will become common during your lifetime?
4. Do you think that Amazon can successfully use drones to deliver packages? Why or why not?
5. Would you like for your president to use AI in decision-making? Why or why not?
6. Could AI be used effectively to match compatible romantic partners?
7. Could AI be used to teach English effectively? Which would you prefer to teach you, AI or a human teacher?

Current Hot Topic: Is Artificial Intelligence a Danger to Humans?

Stephen Hawking, one of the world's preeminent scientists, has warned against the dangers of artificial intelligence. In an interview with the BBC, Hawking said, "The development of full artificial intelligence could spell the end of the human race." He stated that the simple forms of AI that have been developed so far are very useful, but he is fearful of creating AI that surpasses human beings. He added that AI could "take off on its own, and re-design itself at an ever increasing rate. Humans, who are limited by slow biological evolution, couldn't compete and would be superseded."

For Further Discussion:

1. Do you agree with Hawking that AI could be a danger to the human race? Why or why not?
2. What are some tasks that AI could never be capable of doing?

— We need some investment from outside. For that, I want you to do some "window dressing" on our finances.
— What do you mean? Do you want me to rig our accounting?
— All you have to do is change some numbers. That'll be easy, right?
— Yes, it's a piece of cake, but I'm afraid I might be sent to prison. What you're asking is illegal!
— Don't worry! If you do your best, we'll get a lot of investment money, and we'll be able to employ famous lawyers. They'll keep you from being put behind bars.

Topic Preview:

Have you ever read about an accounting scandal in your country? What companies were involved? What happened? What sort of punishment did the participants receive? Would you make false records for your company if your boss asked you to do so?

Dialogue:

Jackson: Chloe, whatever happened to that American fraudster Bernard Madoff?

Chloe: Oh, he's still in prison. He was sentenced to 150 years in prison, so he will never get out.

Jackson: Wow! That's a very harsh sentence! All of that for fraudulent investments?

Chloe: Well, remember that the fraud involved about $65 billion, the largest in U.S. history.

Jackson: Oh, I didn't realize it was that bad.

Chloe: To make matters worse, some charities invested in Madoff's investment program, and some of them had to close their doors due to their losses.

Jackson: How could something like that happen?

Chloe: Well, many people said that the Securities and Exchange Commission did not investigate Madoff's firm properly.

Jackson: It sounds as though the officials didn't do their job. Were they punished too?

Chloe: Not at all. All of those officials are still working in the financial industry.

Accounting Fraud

The job of accounting is often regarded as a very technical and boring profession. However, accountants are very important individuals in the economic life of a country. Accounting measures the successes and failures of a business and presents the resulting data in a form that can be understood by the company's management, as well as investors, creditors, and regulators. Thus, accounting is often called the "language of business." The terms "accounting" and "financial reporting" are often used as synonyms.

The task of accounting is carried out by accountants and auditors, who are expected to adhere to strong ethical principles. If you are considering investing in a company, you will certainly want access to the company's financial statement, which is a report that presents a true and fair picture of the company's financial health. You can only make an informed decision about a company if you have truthful information. Unfortunately, the expected ethical standards of accounting are not always followed. Accountants and auditors must present accurate information to the public and to the government, but at the same time, they have a vested interest in that they would like to remain employed at the company they are auditing. They face a classic case of a conflict of interest.

To see what a lack of ethics in accounting can do to a company's reputation, you need look no further than the firm of Arthur Andersen. Founded in 1913, this company was one of the top five accounting firms in the United States until 2002, when the company was found guilty of criminal charges relating to fraudulent accounting. In 2001, an energy company named Enron had falsely reported that it had earned $100 billion in revenue, and the Arthur Andersen firm had acted with complicity in presenting false financial statements. In addition, the firm was convicted of obstruction of justice for shredding documents related to Enron, which led to the firm losing its license to practice in the field of accounting. With its reputation in shatters, Arthur Andersen ceased to exist as a viable company.

ISSUE 16 ACCOUNTING FRAUD

Vocabulary & Expressions:

regulator
*an official who ensures that companies follow rules and principles that are required by law or ethics
- Government *regulators* ensure that rules of safety are followed in the workplace.

auditor
*a person who examines financial accounts and records, verifies the information, and announces the results
- The local city government hired an *auditor* to ensure that its tax records were correct.

adhere to
*to follow closely or exactly
- The strict teacher demanded that all students *adhere to* his rules.

access to
*the ability, right, or permission to approach, enter, speak with someone, or use some item
- The police department has *access to* every citizen's driving record.

informed decision
*a decision based on facts or information, not on emotion or untruthfulness
- It's difficult for a voter to make an *informed decision* when politicians try to hide their real plans.

vested interest
*a strong personal interest in a situation, system, arrangement, or institution; a personal stake in something
- The principal of a school has a *vested interest* in the success of his students because he could lose his job if they don't do well.

conflict of interest
*a situation in which an official has to make a decision where he might also profit personally
- A judge who makes a decision about a company in which he has invested money has a *conflict of interest*.

look no further
*an expression used to say that what you are offering is exactly what someone is trying to find
- The advertiser said, "If you want a great vacation spot, you need *look no further* than Miami Beach."

complicity
*the situation of being involved with others in crime or wrongdoing; being an accomplice
- Even if you did not commit a crime, you might be charged with *complicity* if you help someone else commit a crime.

obstruction of justice
*to interrupt, hinder, or oppose the course of justice
- The friend of the bank robber was convicted of *obstruction of justice* because he lied to the police.

shred
*to cut or tear into small pieces; reduce to shreds
- Nowadays, most companies have a paper shredder which *shreds* unneeded documents quickly.

in shatters
*broken into small pieces; in pieces and unrepairable
- The athlete was convicted of using drugs, which left his reputation *in shatters*.

viable
*practicable, workable; capable of becoming useful
- On busy highways made only for cars, bicycles are not *viable* forms of transportation.

Let's Talk Business

Discussion Points:

1. Have you ever read about any accounting scandals in your country? What happened?
2. Do you think that accountants who participate in fraud should be sent to prison? For how long?
3. In the U.S., the exam to become a Certified Public Accountant (CPA) is very difficult. Is that true in your country also?
4. If you were an accountant and your boss asked you to create false financial records, what would you do?
5. What academic subjects would be good for an accountant to study?
6. Do you think that accounting is a boring profession? Why or why not?
7. Charles Scott said, "Creativity is great—but not in accounting." What did he mean?

Current Hot Topic: Punishment for Financial Fraud

What is reasonable punishment for someone convicted of accounting fraud? Some prison sentences seem excessive, and others seem too light. In 2009, Bernard Madoff pleaded guilty to operating a fraudulent investment scheme for decades. The amount missing from Madoff's clients' accounts totaled $65 billion, making his crime the largest financial fraud in U.S. history. Madoff was sentenced to 150 years in prison. At the other extreme is the Arthur Andersen case. The accounting firm was convicted of obstruction of justice in the Enron Scandal but ended up with only a five-year probation and a $500,000 fine.

For Further Discussion:

1. Do you think a sentence of 150 years for Madoff is reasonable? Why or why not?
2. Do you think that the prison sentences for financial fraud in your country are reasonable? Why or why not?

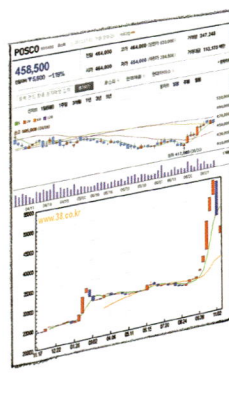

— Whenever I buy stocks, they begin to fall, and whenever I sell them, they begin to go up.
— That's very funny. I always buy stocks that are likely to go up and sell stocks that are supposed to go down.
— Are you kidding? Are you a fortuneteller?
— No, I'm serious.
— I guess you've made a fortune then.
— No, not yet.
— Why not?
— Whenever I make some profits by trading stocks using insider information, the government fines me the same amount of money.

Topic Preview:

What exactly is a "stock" or "share" of a company? How can the average person buy stocks of a certain company? Is investing in stocks a good way to become rich, or are the risks greater than the potential rewards? How do you decide about which stocks to buy?

Dialogue:

Noah: Emma, would you be interested in buying stocks in a new company?

Emma: I'm not sure. What sort of company are you talking about?

Noah: It's a new electronics company that a friend gave me a tip about.

Emma: Oh, that kind of tip almost never works out. There are so many scams in stocks.

Noah: But think about how rich you would be if you had bought stocks in Microsoft when it was first offered.

Emma: Yes, that's true, but for every successful company, there are a hundred that fail.

Noah: Hmmm...you are a very cautious person!

Emma: Yes, I am. I work hard for my money, and I don't want to lose it.

Noah: Okay. You have a point there.

Emma: I will only buy stocks in a well-established company.

The Stock Market

When a corporation is formed, the ownership of the company is divided into stocks, which are also called shares. When a person buys some shares, that person owns a fraction of the business. Investors buy shares in companies usually through two ways. The first and most common method is through a stock exchange. There are currently about 60 stock exchanges in the world, representing companies with a market capitalization of $70 trillion. The largest 16 stock markets account for 87% of the global market. The largest stock market is that of the United States, and the largest stock exchange in the world is the New York Stock Exchange, which is located on Wall Street in New York City. A second method of buying stocks is through an over-the-counter purchase (OTC), which refers to buying shares directly from a dealer.

When a company first offers its shares for sale, the sale is known as an "initial public offering" (IPO). Investors dream of buying cheap shares in a startup company and later selling those shares for a huge sum of money if the company becomes successful. For example, if you had bought 45 shares in Apple when it was first offered in 1980, you would have spent only $990. That investment would be worth more than $300,000 today.

In contrast to the meteoric rise of Apple, most IPOs eventually fail. During the period of 1997 to 2001, investors speculated excessively in any company that was connected to the Internet. However, during the period of 2000-2002, this "dot-com bubble" burst, and many companies went out of business. Many investors lost their shirt. However, stronger companies, such as Ebay and Amazon, survived the dot-com boom and became very successful. Stock markets may also experience a "crash," such as what happened on "Black Monday," October 19, 1987, when markets around the world suddenly lost a huge amount of their value. Because of the risk involved, investing in the stock market is not for the faint-hearted.

ISSUE 17 THE STOCK MARKET

Vocabulary & Expressions:

stock exchange
*a place where shares in companies are bought and sold
- The Korea Exchange is the 15th largest **stock exchange** in the world.

market capitalization
*the total market value of a public company or a stock exchange
- The **market capitalization** of Samsung and all its divisions totals around $400 billion.

account for
*to give an explanation for something
- The teacher asked the student to **account for** his missing homework.

startup
*related to a new business venture or project
- Many **startup** companies fail because of a lack of knowledge or a lack of money.

meteoric
*resembling a meteor in speed or suddenness of appearance
- Emmanuel Macron was a French banker who entered politics and experienced a **meteoric** rise to the presidency.

speculate
*to engage in any business transaction that involves huge risks but with the opportunity for large gains
- You should never **speculate** with money that you cannot afford to lose.

bubble
*a situation with excessive speculation, where prices of items are greater than their real value (e.g., *housing bubble, stock market bubble*)
- The real-estate **bubble** ruined many investors in the mid-2000s.

lose one's shirt
*to lose all that one owns, to suffer a severe financial loss
- He **lost his shirt** by playing roulette in the casino.

boom
*a rapid increase in price or numbers
- Recently there has been a **boom** in housing construction.

faint-hearted
*lacking courage, timid
- Choosing a military career is not for the **faint-hearted**.

Let's Talk Business

Let's Talk Business

Discussion Points:

1. If you wanted to invest some money, would you prefer to invest in stocks, bonds, or real estate?
2. The stocks of the strongest companies are called "blue chips." These stocks are stable but bring small returns on investment (ROI). Would you prefer to invest in dependable blue chips or in high-yielding stocks that also have high risk?
3. There are always ups and downs in the stock market, so everyone tries to "buy low and sell high." However, even people who buy in down markets and sell in up markets often do not make much money. How can we explain this phenomenon?
4. Sometimes individual investors are called "ants" because they move frantically, have little influence, and cannot outperform large institutions. Is there any way that "ants" can make money in the stock market?
5. At present, people can buy stocks on credit, which simply fuels speculation in the market. Do you think the government should prohibit buying stocks on credit? Why or why not?
6. What are the three best stocks to buy in your country?
7. Warren Buffet said, "Enjoy no frequent trading." Can you explain what he meant?

Current Hot Topic: Automated Trading System

In previous generations, stock trades were completed the old-fashioned way. A broker would yell "buy orders" on the stock exchange floor. However, nowadays about 75% of trading orders originate from an automated trading system (ATS), which is also known as "programmed trading." The advantage of this system is that computers can execute buy and sell orders faster than humans and do so without emotion. However, programmed trading has sometimes created large swings in stock prices, leading to instability.

For Further Discussion:

1. Which is more trustworthy for buying stocks, a computer or a human being?
2. Has your country ever experienced a stock market crash? What do you know about it?

I'm driving a car called the economy. To make the economy remain robust, I have to manage interest rates by shifting up and down according to the speed of the car. The most difficult task is timing while shifting. Shifting a bit earlier or later makes the car rattle. The moral of the story is simple: maintaining a healthy economy is as difficult as driving a car safely.

Topic Preview:

Do you have any money in a savings account? Have you ever taken out a loan to buy a house, car, or other item? Do you have a credit card? If you answer yes to any of these questions, then you are certainly aware of how interest rates affect you personally. However, how do you think interest rates affect the national economy?

Dialogue:

William: Isabella, you're majoring in economics, right?

Isabella: Yes, I am. Why do you ask?

William: Well, I've just inherited some money from my grandmother who passed away last year.

Isabella: I'm sorry for your loss. I guess you are concerned now about what to do with the money.

William: Yeah, that's right. I want to invest it but in a conservative approach, so I don't lose any of the money.

Isabella: Well, the most conservative approach is to put the money into a certificate of deposit, or CD.

William: What sort of interest rate could I get on a CD nowadays?

Isabella: The current rate is a little less than 1%.

William: Oh my! That's very low. That's less than the rate of inflation!

Isabella: You're right. Inflation is running around 1.6% now.

William: I'm not sure what to do.

Isabella: Well, if you're willing to take more risk, there's always stocks and real estate.

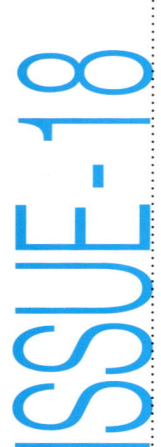

Interest Rates

The word "interest" is a financial term that refers to a sum of money paid for the use of another person's money or simply for borrowing money. The rate of interest is usually expressed as a percentage, called the APR. The amount of interest that you pay for borrowing money from a bank is always higher than the interest rate that the bank pays you when you have a savings account. For example, if you borrow money from a bank to buy a house, you can expect to pay an interest rate of about 4%. However, if you have a savings account at the same bank, they will pay you less than 1% for using the money that is in your savings account.

The current interest rates that you see at your local bank ultimately rest upon the rates set by your country's central bank. The central bank establishes a monetary policy, which takes into account variables such as investments, inflation, and unemployment. As a general policy, central banks reduce interest rates if they want to increase investment and consumption within the national economy. However, if interest rates are too low, they can create a macroeconomic problem. With low interest rates, investors pour large amounts of money into the stock market and the real estate market. Such large-scale investments can create an economic bubble, which will eventually burst. Therefore, in developed economies, interest-rate adjustments are made cautiously and are designed to ensure that economic growth proceeds steadily. If the economy begins to slow down too much, the central bank can adjust interest rates to jump-start the economy.

The most important central bank in the world is the Federal Reserve System of the United States. The "Fed," as it is nicknamed, manages the world's largest economy, which has a total GDP of $18 trillion, almost 25% of the global GDP. Thus, the American central bank has a massive influence on the economies of various countries. As economists say, "When America sneezes, the rest of the world catches a cold."

ISSUE 18 INTEREST RATES

Vocabulary & Expressions:

APR
*abbreviation for "annual percentage rate," a statement of the yearly interest rate for financial transactions
- I just cut up my credit card because the bank raised the *APR* to 21%.

borrow
*to obtain money from a bank for temporary use; not to be confused with its opposite, *lend* (or *loan*), which means to *provide* money for temporary use
- I *borrowed* $500 from Citibank, and they seemed happy to lend it to me.

central bank
*the institution that manages a nation's currency, money supply, and interest rates
- The *central bank* for the Eurozone is known as the European Central Bank (ECB).

monetary policy
*the process by which a central bank controls the supply of money, interest rates, and rate of inflation in order to contribute to economic growth and lower unemployment
- The *monetary policy* of the central bank directly affects interest rates and indirectly affects stock prices.

take into account
*to consider, make allowance for
- Anyone who wants to start a new business needs to *take into account* all the factors that are necessary for success.

variable
*liable to vary or change, changeable
- The weather in Boston is *variable*; it can be sunny one minute and raining the next minute.

inflation
*an economic term referring to a continuing rise in the general level of prices; opposite term: *deflation*
- The average cost of a loaf of bread was only $0.12 in 1950, but in 2013, it was $1.98, all because of *inflation*.

consumption
*the buying of goods and services; from the verb *consume* and related to the noun *consumer*
- When many new jobs become available, people have more money, and *consumption* increases as well.

macroeconomic
*related to the broad and general aspects of the economy of a country as a whole; opposite term: *microeconomic*, related to a specific aspect of the economy, for example, the profit status of one company
- The central bank sets *macroeconomic* policies to help the nation as a whole.

pour
*to send or push something continuously
- The college *poured* a huge amount of money into remodeling the old classroom building.

large-scale
*very extensive, of great scope
- The government proposed a *large-scale* plan for improving social welfare.

jump-start
*to revive or enliven
- The presidential candidate promised that his policies would *jump-start* the slow economy.

Let's Talk Business

Discussion Points:

1. What is the central bank called in your country? Can you explain its main policies? Who is the current governor of the central bank?
2. How is the governor of the central bank chosen in your country? Do you think the process should be changed?
3. Has your country ever gone through a period of high inflation? What happened? How did it affect you?
4. Have you ever had to borrow any money? Where did you borrow the money? What was the interest rate?
5. If you suddenly received a lot of money, would you want to keep it in your country's currency? Why or why not? If you chose another currency, which one would you choose?
6. What is the current APR that people have to pay on credit cards in your country? What is the APR that you can receive on a savings account?
7. Can you explain what this saying means: "When America sneezes, the rest of the world catches a cold"?

Current Hot Topic: Sky-High Interest Rates on Credit Cards

A major complaint by consumers concerns excessively high interest rates charged by banks for credit card use. For example, in the U.S., the interest rate set by the Federal Reserve in 2017 was very low, varying from about 1.0% to 1.25%. In theory, this low rate should result in lower rates for consumers who use credit cards. However, the average credit card interest rate for 2017 was a whopping 15%. Not surprisingly, major banks consistently report huge profits in their operations.

For Further Discussion:

1. Why do banks charge such high rates on credit cards when the banks receive the money at a very low rate of interest?
2. Do you think the government should pass a law that places strict limits on how much interest banks can charge for credit card use?

Importer: Make the US dollar much stronger, so we can import more goods and have stabilized prices.

Exporter: Make the US dollar much weaker, so we can export more goods to other countries, and manufacturers will employ more workers.

They both have a point. Maybe we should just flip a coin.

Topic Preview:

What happens to the economy of your country when the national currency becomes weaker? What happens when the national currency becomes stronger? Does your country's central bank have large holdings in various currencies, such as the Euro, the American dollar, and the Japanese yen? Why would they have holdings in other currencies? Have you ever needed to change money from one currency to another? How did you make the transaction?

Dialogue:

Alex: Emily, have you ever exchanged money from one currency to another?

Emily: Of course. Why? Do you need to exchange some money?

Alex: Yes, I do. I've just gotten a job as an English teacher in Korea, and I'm wondering if I should buy some Korean money before I go there.

Emily: So you want to exchange American dollars for Korean currency?

Alex: Well, I'm just wondering if I should.

Emily: I would recommend that you just take your dollars in cash with you when you go to Korea.

Alex: And exchange dollars into Korean money after I arrive?

Emily: Exactly. You will get a better exchange rate than if you try to make the exchange here in the States.

Alex: I see. Thanks for your advice. How do you know so much about currency exchange?

Emily: I'm majoring in international finance. I'm supposed to know about these things!

Exchange Rates

The term "exchange rate" refers to the ratio at which a unit of the currency of one country can be exchanged for that of another country. If the exchange rate between U.S. dollars and the Euro is expressed with the formula US$1 = €0.852, that means that one U.S. dollar will buy 0.852 euros. The exchange rate can also be expressed with the reverse formula €1 = US$1.174. Exchange rates are determined in the foreign exchange market, where there are two types of exchange rates: the "spot exchange" refers to the current exchange rate; the "forward exchange" rate refers to a rate that is quoted and traded today but which will be delivered at a specific date in the future. Because currency rates fluctuate widely, there is no shortage of currency speculators who try to make a killing in currency trading. Currency trading is continuous, 24 hours a day, except on weekends.

The exchange rate is of crucial importance to countries whose economy relies on exports. If the currency of an exporting country becomes stronger, its products will become more expensive to other countries, and exports will decrease. If the exporting country's currency remains weak, its export market will be strong because its goods are cheap to other countries. Because of this phenomenon, countries try to gain an advantage in international trade by manipulating the value of their currency and keeping it low. Such manipulation usually occurs when a country's central bank intervenes in the foreign exchange market. This type of intervention occurs when a country's central bank buys or sells foreign currency in exchange for its own domestic currency. Through these transactions, the country tries to influence the exchange rate to its own benefit.

In the early 21st century, China was frequently accused of currency intervention and manipulation. Critics claimed that China kept its currency devalued so that its exports would be cheaper to other countries. However, in recent years, this accusation seems unwarranted, and many experts now claim that China's currency is actually overvalued, not undervalued.

ISSUE 19 EXCHANGE RATES

Vocabulary & Expressions:

ratio
*the relation in degree or number between two similar things
- The current *ratio* of the U.S. dollar to the Chinese renminbi is 1:6.6 [read as *one to six point six*].

spot
*the price of goods, currencies, or stocks that are offered for immediate delivery and payment; also known as *spot price*
- The current *spot* price for gold is $41.42 per gram.

fluctuate
*to change continually; shift back and forth
- The price of gold *fluctuates* wildly based on current international events.

no shortage of
*an expression that means there is plenty of something
- There is *no shortage of* small cafés in Paris. (= There are many small cafés in Paris.)

make a killing
*a fast and unusually large financial gain or profit
- Bill bought 1,000 shares of Apple when it was first offered in 1980, and he *made a killing* when he sold it years later.

manipulate
*to manage or influence something or someone skillfully, especially in an unfair manner
- The International Monetary Fund (IMF) tells its members not to *manipulate* their currency exchange rates to gain an unfair competitive advantage over other members.

intervene
*to take action in order to modify the market forces of an economy, especially to maintain the stability of a currency
- The Japanese central bank *intervened* in the currency markets today, selling yen for dollars, because they thought the yen had become too strong.

devalue
*to fix a lower value for a currency
- In 2016, Brazil *devalued* its currency, which made farmers happy because it resulted in higher prices in the international market.

unwarranted
*lacking a good or logical reason for a conclusion or action
- It is *unwarranted* to assume that a student cheated on a test just because she made a perfect score.

overvalued
*to value too highly; put too high a value on
- The couple could not sell their house because they *overvalued* it and asked for too much money.

undervalued
*to value below the real worth; put too low a value on
- Tom just bought 100 shares of Samsung stock because he thinks it's currently *undervalued* and will go up in price soon.

Let's Talk Business

Discussion Points:

1. How often does the central bank in your country intervene to influence the currency exchange rate? Why do they do this?
2. Has your country ever experienced a financial crisis when the value of its currency plunged? What happened?
3. Does the central bank of your country maintain large reserves of currency from other countries? Why or why not?
4. In your country, who gains when the value of your national currency decreases? Who loses?
5. What is the current exchange rate between your national currency and the U.S. dollar? What about the euro?
6. Have you ever bought foreign currency? What was your purpose? How much did you buy?
7. Whose faces are on the paper currency in your country? Why were those individuals chosen?

Current Hot Topic: Currency Speculation: Helpful or Harmful?

Currency speculation occurs when individuals engage in risky financial transactions within currency markets in order to profit from short-term fluctuations of the market value of a currency. This type of speculation is a daily occurrence within international currency exchanges. However, experts argue over whether such speculation is helpful or harmful. Some economists, such as Milton Friedman, have argued that speculators perform an important function in currency markets and actually help stabilize the market. Other economists, such as Joseph Stiglitz, consider currency speculation as harmful. In many countries, currency speculation is considered negatively, as nothing more than gambling, a practice that interferes with economic policy.

For Further Discussion:

1. Do you think currency speculation is helpful or harmful to the national economy in your country? What do economists in your country say about this issue?
2. Would you engage in currency speculation if you knew you could make a large profit? What if you knew your large profit would harm the national economy?

— It's just a trade war. Why did you bring a tank?
— We had no choice. This morning, our car had a flat tire, so we had to bring a tank. It doesn't necessarily mean we should use it.
— Good. Anyway, we want to have a fair FTA with you. Do you agree?
— Yes, we want a "fair" FTA with you too. However, FAIR should be IN OUR FAVOR.

Topic Preview:

Does your country have any free trade agreements, or FTAs? Do you think those agreements have been beneficial to your country's economy? Which industries are most helped by FTAs? Which industries are most harmed by FTAs? Has your country ever been involved in a trade war?

Dialogue:

Charlotte: Michael, you're from Australia, right?

Michael: Yeah, that's right. Why do you ask?

Charlotte: Well, I'm writing an essay on free trade agreements. I'm wondering how successful Australia's free trade agreements are.

Michael: Well, Australia has ten free trade agreements in force at the moment. The first one we signed was with our neighbor, New Zealand, back in 1983.

Charlotte: I see. What others does Australia have?

Michael: We have trade agreements with China, Japan, South Korea, the U.S., and I forget the others.

Charlotte: Well, do most Australians believe that these agreements are helpful to the local economy?

Michael: Yeah, I think most people think that our free trade agreements are beneficial. At least, they prevent trade wars from developing.

Charlotte: But there's always some criticism, right?

Michael: Of course, but I read that 78% of Australian exporters were planning to expand their business because of the FTAs.

Charlotte: I see. Well, it sounds as though the FTAs have been good for Australia.

Trade Wars and Free Trade Agreements

A trade war occurs when two or more countries raise or create tariffs or other trade barriers toward each other. This type of conflict often results as a negative side effect of protectionism. A trade war begins when Country A believes that Country B's trading practices are unfair. If Country A raises tariffs on items it imports from Country B, then Country B will retaliate and raise tariffs on items that it imports from Country A. Trade wars that begin with one type of product can spread to other sectors, and trade wars between two countries can spread to other countries.

Trade wars were common in past generations. However, in 1948, many nations signed a legal agreement called the General Agreement on Tariffs and Trade (GATT), whose purpose was to promote international trade and eliminate trade barriers such as tariffs or quotas. The GATT was replaced by the World Trade Organization (WTO) in 1995. As an intergovernmental organization that regulates international trade, the WTO must sometimes deal with issues of dispute settlement. A dispute occurs when one member country adopts a trade policy or takes some action that another member country considers to be a breach of WTO agreements.

In spite of the WTO's rules, trade disagreements can still occur. For example, in the mid 1990s, the U.S. government approved the production and export of some crops that were genetically modified (GM). A number of European Union (EU) nations banned GM exports from the U.S. as potentially unsafe, even though scientific evidence showed that the crops were safe. In 2003, the U.S. filed a formal complaint with the WTO, alleging that the EU had violated international trade agreements by blocking imports of U.S. farm products. A year later, new GM crops were approved, but GM foods remain controversial, and EU countries can take advantage of opt-out provisions.

In order to facilitate trade and avoid disputes, more and more countries are signing free trade agreements (FTAs). Nowadays, almost half of U.S. exports go to the 20 countries that it has FTAs with.

ISSUE 20 TRADE WARS AND FREE TRADE AGREEMENTS

Vocabulary & Expressions:

tariff
*a tax charged by a government on imports in order to limit imports, raise revenue, and protect national products
- The American president threatened to impose a *tariff* on cheap steel imports from China.

barrier
*anything that restrains or stops access or progress
- Canada, Mexico, and the U.S. signed a free trade agreement called NAFTA, which was designed to eliminate trade *barriers*.

side effect
*a secondary effect of something, especially an undesirable one
- Some people who quit smoking experience the *side effect* of gaining weight.

protectionism
*the practice of imposing taxes on foreign goods in order to protect domestic industries from foreign competition
- Most economists believe that the world economy benefits greatly from free trade, but many countries still have policies of *protectionism*.

sector
*a distinct part of a society or of a nation's economy
- The housing *sector* is expected to improve next year.

quota
*a prescribed number or quantity, for example, of items to be imported or exported, or immigrants admitted to a country
- China currently follows a *quota* system for international films, allowing a maximum of 34 overseas films per year.

intergovernmental
*involving two or more governments or levels of government
- The IPCC is an *intergovernmental* body set up for the purpose of studying climate change.

dispute settlement
*a method of making fair decisions in case of a debate, controversy, or difference of opinion
- The WTO has issued rulings in hundreds of international trade disagreements through its *dispute settlement* procedures.

breach
*a violation of a law, trust, faith, or promise
- The attacks on civilians during the war were a *breach* of international humanitarian law.

opt-out
*having the ability to decide to leave or withdraw
- The free email service contained *opt-out* provisions so users could choose not to receive advertisements.

facilitate
*to make an action or process easier
- Careful planning *facilitates* any kind of project.

free trade agreement
*an agreement between two or more countries to reduce trade barriers, quotas, and tariffs and to increase trade of goods and services with each other; abbreviated as FTA
- Japan and the EU have been negotiating a *free trade agreement* since 2013, but talks have intensified after Donald Trump became the U.S. president.

Let's Talk Business

Let's Talk Business

● Discussion Points:

1. Do you think that the WTO is the best place to resolve trade disputes among nations? Is the WTO truly fair, or does it favor advanced countries?
2. Is it reasonable for the WTO to include opt-out provisions for certain types of exports? How effective are trade laws if countries can simply opt out of them?
3. What countries does your country have FTAs with? Do you think those agreements are fair and beneficial?
4. Are there any countries that you would like to see your country sign an FTA with in the future? What benefits would your country receive?
5. Has your country banned imports of genetically modified foods? Why or why not? Are you willing to eat GM foods?
6. What are your country's greatest exports? What are your country's most common imports?
7. What international products do you buy most often? What are some international products that you never buy?

● Current Hot Topic: Donald Trump's "America First" Policy

When Donald Trump ran for president in 2016, his campaign slogan was "Make America Great Again." Trump also promised that, if he were elected president, he would follow an "America First" policy. Many international observers concluded that Trump might lead the U.S. into a protectionist trade stance. In fact, during Trump's first week in office, he signed a notice that he would withdraw the U.S. from the Trans-Pacific Partnership (TPP). Twelve nations had worked for seven years negotiating the TPP, the largest trade agreement in history, but Trump withdrew the U.S. from the TPP in an instant.

● For Further Discussion:

1. Do you think that Trump's "America First" policy will help the American economy? Why or why not?
2. Has your country's government ever had a policy similar to the "America First" policy? Do you think that citizens of your country should always try to buy locally produced products?

Governor: If you decide to build a factory here, we'll provide the best environment for your business to succeed. First of all, we'll give you land free of charge for your factory, impose no taxes for ten years, and build exclusive expressways for your factory

CEO: Wow! I'm sure we'll succeed in a short time.

Governor: We hope your business will prosper sooner, so we can double your taxes, triple your fees for expressways, and quadruple your land fees.

CEO (talking to himself): I must build a factory with wheels to neutralize their evil plans, so I can move my factory when they turn their back on me.

Topic Preview:

Does your country try to attract foreign companies to open factories or offices locally? What incentives does your country offer for foreign investors, such as low taxes or no taxes? Do you think it's worth it for your government to offer such incentives? Do companies from your country ever move their operations to other countries?

Dialogue:

Amelia: Daniel, does the U.S. have any free trade zones?

Daniel: Yes, we have some. There's one in Miami, where I'm from.

Amelia: Really? How does it work?

Daniel: Well, the Miami Free Zone provides a wholesale marketplace for foreign companies.

Amelia: I see. Can they avoid paying taxes?

Daniel: Yes, they can. They can eliminate duties or delay them.

Amelia: It's surprising to me that a developed country like the U.S. would still be trying to attract investors.

Daniel: Well, even developed countries want more economic investment.

Amelia: I see. Do you know about other free trade zones in the U.S.?

Daniel: I've read about others in Boston, Seattle, and Houston, but I don't know much about them.

Amelia: Okay. Thanks for the information!

Daniel: Anytime.

Attracting Investment

Every country would love to lure other countries into moving their operations or making investments locally, but how can this aim be accomplished? One way is to set up a special economic zone (SEZ). This sort of zone is an area where business and trade laws are different from the rest of the country. In other words, the government makes the trade laws within the SEZ more conducive for attracting foreign direct investment (FDI). Favorable policies are usually enacted in areas such as investing, taxation, trading, customs, and labor regulations. Also, companies may be offered "tax holidays," by which they pay lower taxes or no taxes at all for a certain period. Foreign companies are willing to open factories or offices in SEZs because these zones help the companies to become more competitive globally. The term "special economic zone" covers various types of zones, including free trade zones (FTZ), free economic zones (FEZ), industrial estates (IE), bonded logistics parks (BLP), and urban enterprise zones.

The country that has been the most successful in using SEZs to attract foreign investment is China. In 1980, China established four SEZs, all of which were based in the southeastern coastal region. These areas offer tax incentives to foreign investors, and the cities are allowed to develop their own infrastructure without approval from the central government. Based on the success of its SEZs, China has even declared an entire province, Hainan, to be an SEZ.

Not to be outdone, China's neighbors have also set up SEZs. For example, South Korea established the Incheon Free Economic Zone (IFEZ) in 2003, which consists of the regions of Songdo, Cheongna, and the island of Yeongjong. The IFEZ area is planned to be a self-contained living and business district, with residences, schools, hospitals, shopping, and entertainment facilities. In order to attract international businesses to relocate to the IFEZ, the Korean government promises that no taxes will be levied on corporate and individual income for several years. There will be no property taxes for 10 years, and after that, only 50% of the normal property taxes will be exacted.

ISSUE 21 ATTRACTING INVESTMENT

Vocabulary & Expressions:

lure
*to attract, entice, or tempt
- The politician tried to **lure** voters by promising to lower taxes.

conducive
*helpful to, contributing to, leading to; (usually followed by *to* or *for*)
- Daily exercise is **conducive** to good health.

enact
*to make into a law
- Thousands of bills, or potential laws, are introduced in Congress, but only about 4% of them are **enacted**.

industrial estate
*a special area near a town where there are a lot of factories and businesses; also called *industrial park*
- The government plans to establish an **industrial estate** near the airport next year.

bonded
*a condition in which taxable goods are stored securely without payment of taxes until the goods are withdrawn
- **Bonded** warehouses are under the direct control and supervision of customs officials.

logistics
*the detailed planning, organization, and coordination of any large complex operation
- The **logistics** of hosting a World Cup are enormous.

enterprise
*a project or undertaking, especially one that requires boldness or energy
- Entrepreneurs are always looking for new **enterprises** and opportunities.

infrastructure
*the fundamental facilities and systems serving a country, such as transportation, communication, electrical power, and schools
- The president promised to spend billions on improving **infrastructure**, especially in repairing old bridges.

not to be outdone
*not wanting someone else to do something better than you
- **Not to be outdone** by Walmart, Amazon has begun to sell groceries too.

self-contained
*containing within itself all parts necessary for completeness; self-sufficient
- A fully **self-contained** apartment includes a kitchen, oven, shower, toilet, television, and microwave.

levy
*to impose a tax
- The government **levies** taxes on tobacco to discourage tobacco use and to enhance public health.

income
*the money received by a company or person as payment for goods, services, rents, or investments
- The U.S. government imposed its first personal **income** tax in 1861 to help pay for the war effort in the American Civil War.

exact
*to force or compel the payment of money
- If you borrow money from a bank, you can be sure that they will **exact** payment of the loan.

Let's Talk Business

Let's Talk Business

Discussion Points:

1. Why do you think China has been so successful with its SEZs? Have any companies from your country invested in one of China's SEZs?
2. How many SEZs can you name in your country? Do you think they have been successful in luring international investors?
3. Would you like for your country to declare an entire province as an SEZ? Why or why not? Which province would be the best choice for an SEZ?
4. Is it wrong for developed countries to promote SEZs? Aren't they taking away much-needed opportunities from developing countries?
5. Do you think that SEZs are unfair to local businesses? Why should international investors get tax breaks? Why not just lower taxes for local businesses?
6. If you started a company, would you prefer to start it within another country's SEZ? Why or why not?
7. Have you ever visited an SEZ in your country or another country? What was your experience like?

Current Hot Topic: Special Economic Zones—Worth the Cost?

In mid-2017, the legislature in the U.S. State of Wisconsin voted to give $3 billion in incentives to Foxconn, a Taiwan-based company, if the company would open its first American factory in Wisconsin. In effect, Wisconsin was willing to pay $3 billion to get the 3,000 jobs that Foxconn promised. That means that, in effect, the state will be paying around $1 million per job for the first year. Even when the cost is spread over the next 15 years, the state will still be paying $66,600 per employee, while the employees will have an average salary of $53,000 per year. Many citizens of Wisconsin are asking themselves how this sort of extravagant incentive will help their state in the long run. Every country that opens up an SEZ faces the same sort of question.

For Further Discussion:

1. If you lived in Wisconsin, would you support the deal with Foxconn? Why or why not?
2. Do you think that SEZs are worth the cost in the long run? Why or why not?

Dad: When I was young, the color of the river was blue, but now it is black.
Son: What are you talking about? It's always been black. I've never seen any blue river.
Dad: I remember when it was blue and we didn't wear a mask.
Son: Really? What changed the color of the river into black?
Dad: HUMAN GREED. We have achieved economic development at the expense of the environment. I'm afraid we've crossed the bridge of no return.

Topic Preview:

Is it possible to promote economic development and protect the environment at the same time? Is one goal more important than the other, or are both objectives of equal importance? If a new factory would create 5,000 new jobs in your hometown but would harm the environment, would you support opening the factory? Should developing economies be allowed to ignore environmental problems more than developed nations?

Dialogue:

Samuel: Zoey, which do you think is more important: to promote fast economic development or to protect the environment?

Zoey: Hmmm....I don't think you can say that one is more important than the other.

Samuel: So you think they are of equal importance?

Zoey: Yes, I do, but we cannot sacrifice our environment just to make more money.

Samuel: Well, it sounds as though you think protecting the environment is more important.

Zoey: I think you have to look at "economy versus environment" issues on a case-by-case basis.

Samuel: Oh, I see. So sometimes one issue is more important than the other?

Zoey: Yeah, that's right.

Samuel: Okay. That seems to be a very balanced view.

Zoey: Well, I think so. By the way, why are you so interested in this topic?

Samuel: I'm writing a research paper on the topic. I just wanted to get someone else's opinion.

Economic Development and the Environment

The term "economic development" refers to the process by which a nation improves the economic well-being of its citizens. As a country's economy improves, the social well-being of its people also improves. The topic of economic development is naturally of utmost importance to developing countries whose dream is to achieve the standard of living and quality of life enjoyed in developed countries. However, even in developed countries, politicians promise that, once they are elected, they will take the economy to even greater heights. The terms "economic development" and "economic growth" are somewhat different in meaning. The former concept requires a policy intervention with the aim of improving people's economic and social well-being; the latter idea is a phenomenon of market productivity and rise in GDP.

Almost everyone in the world would agree that improving people's well-being through economic development is an admirable goal. Indeed, the World Bank states that its mission is as follows: "(1) To end extreme poverty by reducing the share of the global population that lives in extreme poverty to 3 percent by 2030. (2) To promote shared prosperity by increasing the incomes of the poorest 40 percent of people in every country." Economic development can help eradicate poverty and hunger, improve education, promote gender equality, reduce child mortality, improve maternal health, and combat HIV/AIDS and other deadly diseases.

Unfortunately, the promotion of economic development often creates clashes with another desirable goal: the aim of protecting the environment. In order to balance the two objectives, the World Bank is also committed to environmental sustainability. Two areas are of particular concern: (1) deforestation, especially in areas of biodiversity; and (2) the increase in greenhouse gas emissions, which lead to a warmer planet. World Bank President Jim Yong Kim has said, "A 4-degree warmer world can, and must be, avoided—we need to hold warming below 2 degrees. Climate change is one of the single biggest challenges facing development, and we need to assume the moral responsibility to take action on behalf of future generations, especially the poorest."

ISSUE 22 ECONOMIC DEVELOPMENT AND THE ENVIRONMENT

Vocabulary & Expressions:

standard of living *the wealth, comfort, material possessions, and necessities available to a certain socioeconomic class; based mostly on one's total income
- Some researchers claim that Finland has the highest *standard of living* in the world.

policy intervention *when the government takes a decisive role in order to modify or determine events or their outcome, especially concerning a country's economy
- A great example of an economic *policy intervention* occurred in 2009 when the U.S. government lent money to the failing auto industry.

market productivity *an economic measure of gains in financial markets
- The phenomenon of *market productivity* is closely connected to labor productivity.

World Bank *an international financial institution that provides loans to various countries of the world for the purpose of economic development
- The *World Bank* has two ambitious goals: to end extreme poverty within a generation and to boost shared prosperity.

gender equality *the condition when all human beings, both men and women, are free to develop their personal abilities and make choices without the limitations set by stereotypes, rigid gender roles, and prejudices
- *Gender equality* has not been achieved yet in the U.S. because women earn only 83% of what men earn.

child mortality *the death of infants and children under the age of five; also known as *under-5 mortality* or *child death*
- The leading causes of a high rate of *child mortality* are pneumonia, preterm birth, diarrhea, malaria, and malnutrition.

sustainability *the quality of not being harmful to the environment or using up natural resources
- Environmental *sustainability* occurs when economic development does not harm the ability of future generations to meet their own needs.

deforestation *the clearance or removal of a forest where the land is afterward converted to a non-forest use
- Some experts claim that *deforestation* has already wiped out roughly 90% of West Africa's original forests.

biodiversity *the number, variety, and genetic variation of different organisms found within a specific geographic region
- Environmentalists consider preservation of *biodiversity* as a major goal of environmental policy.

greenhouse gas *any gases, such as carbon dioxide, methane, nitrous oxide, and ozone, that raise the temperature of Earth's surface
- Without *greenhouse gases*, the average temperature of Earth's surface would be about -18°C, rather than the present average of 15°C.

Let's Talk Business

Let's Talk Business

Discussion Points:

1. Balancing economic development and environmental protection is tricky. Which do you think should be the top priority in your country?
2. Do politicians in your country usually promise to improve economic development?
3. Do you think we should continue to develop nuclear energy technology in spite of the problems involved?
4. Would you support the construction of a new factory if you knew it would significantly harm the environment?
5. The Amazon tropical rain forest is disappearing. What should the rest of the world, especially the developed countries, do in response?

Read the following quotes about the environment.
What do they mean? Do you agree with the idea expressed?

6. We are the last generation with a real opportunity to save the world. Laurence Overmire
7. We do not inherit the earth from our ancestors; we borrow it from our children. Native American proverb

Current Hot Topic: Climate Change Denial

Climate change denial, or global warming denial, involves denial, dismissal, or extreme doubt concerning the scientific opinion on climate change. Climate deniers dispute the extent to which global warming is caused by humans and its impacts on nature and human society. About 97% of scientists believe that human beings are responsible for global warming, so the consensus of the scientific community is clear. However, there are still some politicians who either deny that the climate is becoming warmer, or they claim that it is a natural phenomenon not caused by humans. For example, U.S. Senator Jim Inhofe has called climate change "the greatest hoax ever perpetrated against the American people." Inhofe was one of 22 senators who urged President Donald Trump to withdraw the U.S. from the Paris Agreement, whose purpose is to reduce greenhouse gas emissions. On June 1, 2017, Trump announced that the U.S. would withdraw from the agreement.

For Further Discussion:

1. Is climate change denial an issue in your country? Do you know anyone who is a climate change denier?
2. Do you think that climate change is affecting your country? In what ways?

— Wow! You have four children!
— Yes, we have four but the government is using incentives to encourage us to have even more kids. Now they give us $1,000 monthly for each child, and additionally provide a house, car, and free utilities.
— That's not fair! The government taxes my salary by 50 percent because I'm single.
— Why don't you marry and have children?
— I can't afford to with my job. I just make minimum wage.
— Don't worry. I have no regular job but the government supports me. Now I think child rearing is my MAIN JOB, and MY WIFE IS EXPECTING AGAIN!

Topic Preview:

Why aren't young couples having more children? How will a declining birth rate affect the economy in the future? How will increasing lifespans affect the economy? Will the pension plans that young people are paying into now actually be available when they retire?

Dialogue:

Natalie: Dylan, did you read this article about the declining birth rate in Korea?

Dylan: What article is that?

Natalie: It's an article from the *Chosun Ilbo*, and the title is "Koreans to Become Extinct in 2750."

Dylan: Wow! That's a shocking title! What does the article say?

Natalie: It says that the Korean birth rate is so low that Koreans will disappear by 2750.

Dylan: That's unbelievable! What support is there for such an incredible claim?

Natalie: Well, the article quotes David Coleman, a professor of demography at Oxford.

Dylan: Hmmm…well, if he's from Oxford, he must know what he's talking about.

Natalie: Yeah, he has done demographic studies that show that Korea's population will shrink to 10 million by 2136 and become extinct by 2750.

Dylan: Is the Korean government doing anything to encourage couples to have more children?

Natalie: Yeah, they're trying to increase the birth rate, but they've had very little success.

Demographics and the Economy

Demography is the academic field that studies the vital statistics and social statistics of a country, city, or other group of people, including statistics about births, deaths, diseases, education, marriages, incomes, and similar matters. Demographers typically produce reams of data, which are called *demographics*. If you have ever wondered why McDonald's restaurants are so successful and almost never close, you can find the answer in demographics. Before the company opens a new restaurant, they conduct a demographic study of the target area. If the demographics meet certain parameters, the company will open a new restaurant, and its success will be almost guaranteed.

Almost every national government has a branch that maintains important statistics. It is usually called the Bureau of Vital Statistics, or something similar. The bureau maintains voluminous records that are available to companies, researchers, the media, and the general public. In recent years, two types of statistics have become momentous for many nations: the *birth rate* and the *fertility rate*. The birth rate is the total number of births per 1,000 of a population in a calendar year. The fertility rate of a population is the average number of children that a woman will likely give birth to during her lifetime.

In order for developed countries to sustain their population levels, the fertility rate needs to be at least 2.1 children per woman. If this level is achieved, countries will experience zero population growth. Some industrialized countries consistently fall below this level into a level known as sub-replacement fertility, including the U.S.A. (1.9), Canada (1.6), Germany (1.4), Japan (1.4), Spain (1.3), Portugal (1.2), and South Korea (1.2). The situation in South Korea is particularly acute. In 2017, the growth of South Korea's population will be the slowest rate ever recorded. The Korean government has spent about $70 billion over the past decade trying to boost the country's birth rate. A low birth rate decreases the number of people in the workforce, drives up welfare costs for the expanding elderly population, and undermines future economic growth.

ISSUE 23 DEMOGRAPHICS AND THE ECONOMY

Vocabulary & Expressions:

vital statistics
*data concerning live births, deaths, fetal deaths, diseases, marriages, and divorces
- Issuing birth certificates is one aspect of maintaining a country's *vital statistics*.

social statistics
*data collected to study human behavior in a social environment
- The use of *social statistics* helps answer questions such as "How are populations growing?" and "Are wealthy people happier?"

ream
*a standard quantity of paper, consisting of 500 sheets or 516 sheets; plural *reams*, a large quantity of something
- The romantic young man wrote *reams* of poetry for his girlfriend.

parameters
*limiting factors, boundaries, or guidelines
- The president explained the basic *parameters* of his foreign policy.

bureau
*an office or agency, especially a governmental agency providing services for the public
- Every ten years, the U.S. Census *Bureau* counts every resident in the United States.

voluminous
*capable of filling a volume or volumes
- Most of Thomas Jefferson's political ideas are found in his *voluminous* correspondence.

momentous
*of great or far-reaching importance
- Getting married is certainly one of the most *momentous* days of a person's life.

fertility
*the ability to produce babies
- In 2017, the US fertility rate dropped to the lowest number ever reported since *fertility* records first began to be kept more than a century earlier.

sustain
*to keep up, keep going, or prolong, especially an action or process
- Shy people cannot usually *sustain* any lengthy conversation.

zero population growth
*a condition in which a population neither increases nor decreases because the number of births in a year equals the number of deaths
- China is expected to experience a *zero population growth* rate by 2030.

sub-replacement fertility
*a fertility rate that leads to each new generation having fewer people than the previous one
- In developed countries, *sub-replacement fertility* is any rate below approximately 2.1 children born per woman, but the rate can be as high as 3.4 in some developing countries.

acute
*of extreme importance; crucial, critical
- The U.S. will face an *acute* shortage of airplane pilots over the next two decades.

Let's Talk Business

Discussion Points:

1. Do you think it's important for countries to maintain zero population growth? Why or why not?
2. Why do some countries, like South Korea and Japan, have such a low birth rate?
3. Do you think that Koreans will actually disappear by 2750 and the Japanese by 3100, as some experts predict?
4. What measures has your government tried in order to increase the birth rate?
5. Is it fair to impose heavy taxes on single people in order to increase the birth rate?
6. What could your government do to motivate you and your spouse to have four or more children?
7. Do you know any people who have had more than four children? Do you admire such people or do you think they made a foolish decision?

Current Hot Topic: Increasing Population through Immigration

South Korea is almost 97% ethnic Korean, and Japan is about 98% ethnic Japanese. Because these countries are composed of such homogeneous ethnic groups, they tend to equate nationality or citizenship with racial identity. Also, they often view multiracial and multiethnic nations, such as the U.S. and Canada, as odd or contradictory. Since both South Korea and Japan have low birth rates that could eventually lead to their extinction, should these countries welcome more foreigners into their midst as a way of increasing their population? While both countries have loosened immigration policies slightly, they do not seem enthusiastic about using immigration as a means of counteracting their low birth rates.

For Further Discussion:

1. Do you think that South Korea and Japan should promote immigration as a way of enlarging their population? Why or why not?
2. If you were the national leader of Korea or Japan, what policies would you promote to deal with the problems of a low birth rate?

I want to make lots of friends. But I don't know where to go. Some people say Facebook is good, but others advise me to use Twitter.

I plan to use both of them and make thousands of friends. If all of them buy a car from me, I'll be a millionaire overnight.

I stopped using SNS when I realized the friends I've made through it are pseudo-friends. So I said goodbye to them and decided to enjoy myself with my motorcycle.

Topic Preview:

Has any company ever contacted you through social media? Have you ever responded to a company through social media? If one of your social media friends asks you to "like" the page of a business or organization, do you usually click "like"? How can social media and social networking help a business?

Dialogue:

Henry: Anna, do you have a Facebook account?

Anna: Yes, I do, but I haven't posted very much.

Henry: So, you are not an active user?

Anna: Not at all. I'm not a big fan of social media, actually.

Henry: Why not?

Anna: I used to be more active on social media, but I got tired of friends continually asking me to click "like" on certain pages.

Henry: Oh, you don't enjoy that?

Anna: No, I don't. I'd rather use social media just to keep in touch with my family and to see pictures of my nieces.

Henry: I see. So you don't use Facebook to contact companies or see new products?

Anna: No, I don't. I realize that many people do that and that I'm in the minority.

Henry: Yeah, most companies now have a social media presence, and they use it for marketing their products.

Anna: That's so true, but it's just not for me.

Social Networking and Business

Nowadays, the influence of social media is pervasive. One study revealed that 84% of adolescents in the U.S. have a Facebook account. Some of the most popular online platforms boast millions and even billions of users, as shown by the following user statistics: Facebook, 2,047,000,000; YouTube, 1,500,000,000; WhatsApp, 1,200,000,000; WeChat, 938,000,000; Instagram, 700,000,000; and Twitter, 328,000,000. Most individuals use these electronic avenues to keep in touch with family and friends. However, social media can also be used for business purposes.

The most noticeable business use of social media lies in the area of highly targeted advertising. With social media, for the first time in the business world, it is possible for a business to focus its advertising directly to the exact customers that it wants. Large financial institutions, including Visa and MasterCard, are using Facebook to reach millennials in highly effective ways. Tech-savvy real estate agents are increasing their business through ads that are closely linked to specific locations and zip codes.

Businesses are also using social media to create organic marketing. The earliest Internet advertising was based on the pay-per-click (PPC) model or the banner ad model. Many consumers disliked these approaches because they represented an in-your-face style. However, with social media, businesses can engage in conversations directly with consumers. Restaurants, for example, can deal openly with a customer's complaint by admitting fault and making it right. This sort of transparency helps a business retain customers and gain new ones.

Social media platforms also provide companies with a means of offering real-time, around-the-clock customer service. The company does not have to make a heavy investment in hiring many people; it only has to have to a social media presence.

Another advantage of using online media sites is that they offer companies flexibility in content marketing. Traditional options for publishing new content were time-consuming and costly, but with social media, companies can share content directly and cheaply with consumers. For example, Cisco, a giant tech firm, saved $100,000 on a new product launch by using social media instead of traditional channels.

ISSUE 24 SOCIAL NETWORKING AND BUSINESS

Vocabulary & Expressions:

social media — *websites that are used by large groups of people to share information and to develop social and professional contacts
- Many businesses are using *social media* to find new customers.

platform — *a place for releasing or discussing information publicly; a forum
- Many universities now offer courses through online *platforms*.

avenue — *a means of access or approach
- The young man explored every *avenue* to finance his college education.

millennial — *a person born in the 1980s or 1990s, especially in the U.S.; a member of Generation Y
- *Millennials* are usually more liberal in social and political views than their parents.

savvy — *experienced, knowledgeable, and well-informed; shrewd
- Tech-*savvy* consumers use the Internet to compare prices.

organic — *developing naturally
- *Organic* change that arises naturally among employees may help a business more than planned change directed by top management.

pay-per-click — *an Internet advertising model by which the advertiser pays a small fee to the website owner each time a user clicks on an ad
- *Pay-per-click* advertising is most commonly associated with search engines, such as Google.

banner ad — *an advertisement that appears across the top or bottom or along the side of a web page
- Many Internet users regard *banner ads* as annoying because they distract from a web page's actual content.

in-your-face — *bold, direct, aggressive, and confrontational; done in a direct, often rude way that is annoying and cannot be ignored
- Most people do not like an *in-your-face* style of politics.

make it right — *to fix an unfair situation; to compensate someone for an error or offense
- I found a hair in my soup, but the restaurant apologized and *made it right* by giving me a free meal.

transparency — *openness, accountability, integrity, especially in a business or government
- Governments that show a lack of *transparency* are often very corrupt and characterized by bribery and other financial abuses.

real-time — *at the actual time during which a process or event occurs; instantaneous
- "Live streaming" is a type of *real-time* broadcasting where the viewer sees the images as they are recorded.

around-the-clock — *continuing without pause or interruption; 24 hours a day
- Nurses provided the sick patient with *around-the-clock* care.

content marketing — *online marketing that distributes valuable free content directly to the target audience
- The goal of *content marketing* is to build trust with potential customers, not to sell to them directly.

Let's Talk Business

Let's Talk Business

Discussion Points:

1. In your opinion, how effective are social media accounts used for business purposes?
2. Do you think that companies are too concerned about focusing their advertising on millennials? Why or why not?
3. Have you ever "liked" the social media page of a company? Why or why not?
4. Have you ever bought a product that you first saw advertised on social media? What sort of product was it?
5. Do you like it when your friends recommend that you click on certain Internet pages? Why or why not?
6. Do you ever post reviews of restaurants or other businesses online? Are your reviews usually positive or negative?
7. Which social media platforms do you use most often (e.g., Facebook, YouTube, Twitter)? How much of your social media use involves business purposes?

Current Hot Topic: Social Media Backlash

While social media can help companies promote new products and connect directly with customers, it can also quickly cause a backlash, or sudden negative reaction, if the company makes inappropriate or offensive posts. Mistakes made on social media are highly visible and spread quickly. For example, in 2016, Seoul Secret, a Thai cosmetics company started a new online advertising campaign for a skin-lightening makeup with the slogan "White makes you win." The ad showed a 50-second video of actress and singer Chris Horwang talking about how her white skin helped her to become successful. The ad was met with immediate worldwide criticism as being racist. The company quickly apologized and removed all content related to the video. Because of the potential for making damaging posts, some companies have chosen to abandon social media altogether.

For Further Discussion:

1. Have you ever read about any situations where companies made offensive posts on social media? What happened? Was the company able to recover?
2. Can you think of any large companies that do not have a social media presence? Why do you think they choose to avoid social media?

Mr. Bankrupt: I started my business ten years ago and have run my business LAWFULLY. I paid the required taxes, offered no bribes, and fully followed all governmental guidelines. Then I went bankrupt. I still don't know why.

Reporter: How about you? How did you succeed?

Mr. Success: I've run my business LAWFULLY too, paying plenty of taxes and observing governmental guidelines. However, I became a successful businessman.

Reporter: What's the difference between the two of you?

Mr. Success: I guess the only reason he failed is that he wasn't good at finding LOOPHOLES.

Topic Preview:

Do you think that businesses in your country generally follow ethical guidelines? How often do you read about a businessperson caught in an ethical scandal? Can you think of any businesspersons who went to prison because of ethical violations? Are courses on business ethics required for business majors at universities in your country?

Dialogue:

Andrew: Layla, I hear that your father is a stock broker.

Layla: Yeah, that's right. Why do you ask?

Andrew: I was just wondering if he might have some inside tips about good stocks to buy.

Layla: I'm sure he has some great tips, but they are based on public information.

Andrew: No inside information?

Layla: Of course not! It's unethical and illegal for people to make stock trades based on inside information.

Andrew: But it goes on all the time.

Layla: True, but the people who are caught doing it are sent to prison.

Andrew: So, I guess that means I won't be getting any stock tips from your dad.

Layla: Well, not any tips based on inside information. All of his tips are based on publicly available information. That's the only ethical way to offer stock tips.

Business Ethics

In 2009, hedge fund manager Raj Rajaratnam was riding high. The Sri-Lankan-American had earned an M.B.A. degree from the prestigious Wharton School of the University of Pennsylvania, the same school that Warren Buffet and Elon Musk graduated from. Rajaratnam had become a billionaire by trading stocks through the Galleon Group, a company that he had founded in 1997. However, Rajaratnam's world came crashing down on October 16, 2009, when he was arrested by the FBI for insider trading. After two years of investigation, he was found guilty on 14 counts of conspiracy and securities fraud. He was sentenced to 11 years in prison and fined over $150 million. Prosecutors said that Rajaratnam had made more than $60 million through insider trading in stocks such as Ebay and Google. He is currently in prison and will not be eligible for release until 2021.

Because of ethical lapses like that of Rajaratnam, most business schools now require that their students undergo intensive study of business ethics, which is also known as "corporate ethics." Harvard Business School is a case in point. The school describes its teaching of ethics as follows: "The teaching of ethics here is explicit, not implicit, and our Community Values of mutual respect, honesty and integrity, and personal accountability support the HBS learning environment."

The concern for business ethics became prominent in the United States during the early 1970s, leading to the formation of organizations designed to promote ethics. For example, the Society for Business Ethics was founded in 1980. Among its aims are the following: "Provide a forum in which moral, legal, empirical, and philosophical issues of business ethics may be openly discussed and analyzed." By the mid-1980s, at least 500 courses in business ethics were being offered in the U.S., with about 40,000 students. In 1987, the European Business Ethics Network was founded and stated its mission as follows: "Our mission is to promote ethics and excellence in businesses, to increase awareness about ethical challenges in the global marketplace and to enable dialogue on the role of business in society."

ISSUE 25 BUSINESS ETHICS

Vocabulary & Expressions:

hedge fund *a largely unregulated, speculative mutual fund which offers large returns for high-risk investments
- *Hedge funds* are made available only to certain wealthy investors and cannot be offered to the general public.

riding high *enjoying success
- In 1997, J. K. Rowling published her first book in the Harry Potter series, and she has been *riding high* ever since.

M.B.A. *Master of Business Administration; also written as *master's degree in business administration*
- The *M.B.A.* degree originated in the United States in the early 20th century when companies began to seek scientific approaches to management.

insider trading *the illegal practice of buying and selling of stocks by persons acting on secret information ("inside information") not available to the general public
- The investment banker was sentenced to three years in prison for *insider trading*.

count *a distinct, separate charge in a criminal indictment by a prosecutor
- The CEO faced eight charges of conspiracy and fraud; he was found guilty on three *counts* and not guilty on the other five.

conspiracy *an agreement by two or more persons to commit a crime, fraud, or other illegal act
- A group of individuals can be convicted of *conspiracy* to commit burglary even if the actual burglary never happens.

securities *assets that can be traded, especially stocks and bonds
- The Securities and Exchange Commission (SEC) is the government agency that enforces the *securities* laws in the U.S.

lapse *a moral failure; a change that results in worse behavior
- The politician was not reelected because of his *lapse* of judgment.

case in point *a relevant example of something under discussion; an example that illustrates a point that someone is making
- The harder you work, the more successful you will be; Steve Jobs is a *case in point*.

explicit *clearly and directly expressed or demonstrated; leaving nothing implied or indirect
- The teacher gave *explicit* instructions to the students about the test so that there would be no confusion.

implicit *not explicitly expressed; implied, indirect
- Though not stated directly, the president's comments showed *implicit* criticism of Congress.

accountability *an obligation or willingness to accept responsibility or to account for one's actions
- The politician lacked any sense of *accountability*; he simply blamed others for his own mistakes.

Let's Talk Business

Discussion Points:

1. Do you think that Raj Rajaratnam deserved the lengthy prison sentence that he received? Why or why not?
2. Some economists say that insider trading should be legal. What do you think of this opinion?
3. Are ethics courses required for business majors at universities in your country? Do you think such courses actually help prevent unethical behavior?
4. What are the most well-known cases of business ethics failures in your country? Did the people involved go to prison?
5. Does your company or school have a code of ethics? What sort of rules does it include?

Read the following quotes about ethics.
What do they mean? Do you agree with the idea expressed?

6. Corruption is both a major cause and a result of poverty around the world. Anup Shah
7. Another word for corruption is injustice. Auliq-Ice

Current Hot Topic: Transparency International—How Transparent?

Transparency International (TI), founded in 1993, is a well-known organization that leads the fight against unethical practices in government and business. Each year, the organization publishes its Corruption Perceptions Index (at transparency.org), which provides corruption scores for almost every country in the world. The scores range from 0 (highly corrupt) to 100 (very clean). For 2018, Denmark was ranked the least corrupt country, with a score of 88. Somalia was ranked the most corrupt country, with a score of only 10. Incredibly, TI itself has been criticized for not following its own ethical guidelines. TI's policies prohibit the organization from accepting money from corporations that have been involved in corruption. In spite of that provision, in January 2015, it was reported that TI had accepted a $3 million donation from the German company Siemens, which had earlier paid one of the largest corporate corruption fines in history—$1.6 billion—for paying bribes to government officials in many countries. One TI insider said, "This really shows that Transparency International is not as pure as people think."

For Further Discussion:

1. Do you know your country's ranking on TI's Corruption Perceptions Index? Do you think it is accurate?
2. Do you think it was ethical for TI to accept $3 million from Siemens? Why or why not?

Issue 25 ○ Business Ethics

> I've hacked your computer networks. If you don't send me one million dollars, your system will be destroyed.

> That's great! We've recently built a new firewall that we're sure no hackers can penetrate. It's a good opportunity to test our wall. Go ahead!

> Okay, I'll send the money immediately. Please leave our system uncompromised.

> One million dollars? We can't afford it. We have no choice but to report you to the police!

Topic Preview:

How can companies protect their data from cyberattacks and ransomware? How common are ransomware attacks? Should victims of ransomware pay hackers or just ignore them? What compensation should companies offer customers whose personal information is hacked?

Dialogue:

Luke: Hannah, I just read that Equifax's computer systems were hacked.

Hannah: Yeah, it's terrible. The hackers got access to the personal information of almost half of U.S. citizens.

Luke: Do you know if your information was stolen?

Hannah: Not yet. However, Equifax is one of the largest consumer credit reporting agencies, so there's a good chance that my information was hacked.

Luke: Is the government going to punish Equifax?

Hannah: Lawmakers keep talking about what to do next, but so far, they have not done anything.

Luke: It just seems so unfair.

Hannah: Oh, absolutely! Equifax has access to our personal information, and they use it without our permission, but they cannot even protect our privacy!

Luke: Yes, it's terrible. I'm glad that I live in New Zealand.

Hannah: Well, you're lucky, but your information could get hacked in the future.

Security from Cyberattacks

The word *cyberattack* (or *cyber attack*) refers to an attempt to damage, disrupt, or gain unauthorized access to a computer or computer system for malicious purposes. Cyberattacks vary in type and purpose. First, indiscriminate cyberattacks may be directed at business or government computer systems for the purpose of financial greed. The WannaCry ransomware attack began on May 12, 2017, and within a day had affected more than 230,000 computers in over 150 countries, including those of the U.K.'s National Health Service. The hackers demanded that infected companies pay a ransom to a Bitcoin address in order to have their data restored. Fortunately, a 22-year-old web security researcher from England discovered a kill switch in the ransomware, and he was able to eliminate the threat.

A second type of cyberattack is simply designed to be destructive in nature. For example, the Stuxnet computer worm, first discovered in 2010, has been most often described as an American-Israeli cyberweapon, which caused substantial damage to Iran's nuclear program. Neither Israel nor the U.S. has admitted responsibility for the attacks. Another destructive attack occurred in July 2009 when hackers conducted a series of coordinated cyberattacks against major government sites, news media, and financial websites in South Korea and the United States. North Korea was blamed for the attacks, but the claim was never proven definitively.

Another type of cyberattack is conducted for purposes of espionage. In 2008, the U.S. Department of Defense was attacked by a computer worm named agent.btz, which opened backdoors that allowed access to the computer's data. The worm spread through thousands of computers and took 14 months to eradicate. Computer espionage may also be directed toward business computers. In 2014, a hacker group successfully hacked the computer system of Sony Pictures and released personal information about the company's employees and their families. The hackers demanded that Sony pull its film *The Interview*, a comedy about assassinating North Korean leader Kim Jong-un. Therefore, many experts attributed the attack to North Korea.

Governments and businesses have no choice but to pay billions of dollars each year for cybersecurity. Anyone preparing to start a globalized business must devote substantial funds to this purpose.

ISSUE 26 SECURITY FROM CYBERATTACKS

Vocabulary & Expressions:

disrupt — *to cause disorder or turmoil
- An angry protestor *disrupted* the president's news conference.

unauthorized — *lacking permission; not having official permission
- A man was arrested after he went through a door marked "*unauthorized* access prohibited."

malicious — *motivated by a wrongful desire to inflict injury, harm, or suffering on another; intentionally harmful or spiteful
- The movie star was angry about the *malicious* gossip being spread about him.

indiscriminate — *lacking careful choice; haphazard or random
- Medical experts say that the *indiscriminate* use of antibiotics can cause serious health problems.

ransomware — *malware planted illegally by a hacker in a computer, which disables access to the data until the computer's owner pays a sum of money to the hacker
- To avoid being a victim of *ransomware*, you should update your computer's operating system as soon as updates are issued.

Bitcoin — *a worldwide digital currency and payment system that operates without a central administrator
- As of February 2015, over 100,000 merchants and vendors accepted *Bitcoin* as payment.

kill switch — *a safety mechanism used to turn off machinery or computer systems when they cannot be shut down in the usual manner
- Apple recently announced that it would be adding a *kill switch* feature to future phones.

cyberweapon — *a malware computer program used for military objectives
- Some countries have developed a *cyberweapon* that will shut down an enemy's electrical power grids.

espionage — *the systematic use of spies to obtain secret information, especially by governments to discover military secrets or by companies to discover information about a competitor
- Mr. Sterling, a CIA officer, was convicted of *espionage* because he gave secret information to a newspaper reporter.

worm — *a malware computer program that has the ability to copy itself from machine to machine with the intent of causing them harm
- A computer virus spreads through human activity (such as running a program or opening a file), but a computer *worm* has the ability to spread automatically without human initiation.

eradicate — *to remove or destroy completely
- Smallpox is widely regarded as the only infectious disease ever to be *eradicated*.

pull — *to withdraw or remove
- The publisher *pulled* the book from sale because it contained too many errors.

Let's Talk Business

Let's Talk Business

Discussion Points:

1. Do you think it's possible for experts to design computer software that cannot be hacked?
2. When a company is hacked and customers' personal information is stolen, should that company be punished? What sort of punishment should they receive?
3. Have any countries ever used a cyberweapon against your country? What happened?
4. Have any major companies in your country ever been hacked? What happened?
5. Should Bitcoin be prohibited because it is used by hackers to receive ransom money?
6. Has your personal information ever been hacked? What happened?
7. What sort of virus protection do you use on your computer? How often do you update it?

Current Hot Topic: Cyberattacks to Influence Elections

In 2016, in a major election upset, Donald Trump defeated Hillary Clinton to become President of the United States. Subsequent investigations by many U.S. agencies, including the CIA and FBI, concluded with high confidence that the Russian government had interfered in the presidential election in order to help Trump win. The interference included releasing personal information about Clinton that was gained through hacking as well as spreading fake news on social media that was harmful to Clinton. In 2017, two days before France's presidential election, hackers leaked nine gigabytes of emails from candidate Emmanuel Macron's campaign. Once again, Russia was blamed for the hacking and release of private information. If the intent of the hackers was to hurt Macron's chances of winning the election, their aims were a total failure. Macron won easily with 66% of the vote. Russian officials have repeatedly denied involvement in hacking or leaking with respect to the U.S. or French presidential elections.

For Further Discussion:

1. Who do you think hacked the U.S. and French presidential elections? Was the hacking state-sponsored? What punishment should the hackers receive?
2. Have politicians or election-related websites in your country ever been hacked? What happened?

Railroads are very important infrastructure. Trains can move large amounts of freight at once, and they are relatively safe.

Highways are the industrial arteries of a country's economy. They also reduce the cost of public transportation.

Airplanes are the fastest means of transportation and need no railways except some runways. Of all the transportation systems, it is the most economical.

Bridges are as important as highways and railroads and connect the mainland to the islands. Without them, the mainland and islands couldn't have a balanced economic development.

Topic Preview:

How often do you think about the infrastructure in your country? Do you think the current infrastructure is sufficient or needs improvement? What happens when the infrastructure of a country collapses, for example, during a natural disaster? Would you be willing to pay higher taxes in order to have a stronger infrastructure?

Dialogue:

Audrey: Carter, I'm so sorry to hear about the hurricane that hit the United States.

Carter: Well, thanks for your concern. It didn't do much damage to the mainland U.S., but it hit Puerto Rico very hard.

Audrey: Puerto Rico? Is that part of the U.S.?

Carter: Yes, of course. It's an island in the Caribbean Sea, but all its residents are U.S. citizens.

Audrey: I see. Well, what sort of damage did the hurricane do?

Carter: It made a direct hit on Puerto Rico, knocking out the electrical system for the entire island.

Audrey: Oh my! That must have created havoc for everyone!

Carter: Yes, the infrastructure was not very strong to begin with and was almost completely destroyed.

Audrey: That's so sad.

Carter: Yes, it is. Some hospitals don't have electricity, and patients have died. Ships have arrived with aid, but they can't get it delivered to the people.

Audrey: That's terrible! I guess it will take years to rebuild the island's infrastructure.

Carter: You're absolutely right about that.

Infrastructure

The word "infrastructure" refers to the basic facilities and systems that serve a country or city, including roads, bridges, tunnels, water supplies, sewers, electrical grids, and telecommunication systems (including Internet connectivity). Sometimes the term "critical infrastructure" is used to refer to the most important systems that are absolutely necessary for a city or country to function properly. For example, bridges and highways are essential for people to evacuate a city in the case of a natural disaster, so these aspects would certainly be considered part of the critical infrastructure of a city.

Infrastructure may be owned and managed by governments or by private companies. Generally, most roads, ports, airports, water systems, and sewage networks are publicly owned. Such networks are paid for by taxes, tolls, or user fees. On the other hand, most energy and telecommunications networks are privately owned. The use and development of these networks is paid by the consumers who use them.

Improvements to the infrastructure can be made through public investment or private investment. In 2004, South Korea was in need of a high-speed rail line to cover the 412 km from Seoul to Busan. The Korean government gave the responsibility of constructing the line to the Korean High Speed Rail Construction Authority, a public entity, which was able to complete the new rail line successfully. A different approach was taken by the Taiwan government in 1998 when the country was in need of a high-speed rail line to traverse the 345-km distance from Taipei to Kaohsiung. The government awarded the contract to the Taiwan High Speed Rail Corporation, a private organization, with a 35-year concession contract.

The issue of infrastructure is crucial when a nation places a bid to host an international event, such as the Olympics or World Cup. Because South Korea built up its infrastructure to host the 10th Asian Games in 1986 and again for the 1988 Summer Olympics, it was able to bid successfully for the 2002 World Cup and became a co-host with Japan.

ISSUE 27 INFRASTRUCTURE

Vocabulary & Expressions:

sewer
*a drain or pipe, especially one that is underground, used to carry away waste matter (sewage) or surface water
- The New York *sewer* system contains 6,600 miles (10,622 km) of pipes.

grid
*a system of electrical distribution serving a large area, especially by means of high electrical lines
- Hurricane Maria knocked out the entire electrical *grid* of Puerto Rico in 2017.

telecommunication
*the transmission of information, especially words, sounds, or images, usually over great distances, in the form of electromagnetic signals
- The most common *telecommunication* systems are telephone, radio, and television.

connectivity
*a computer term referring to the ability to link to and communicate with other computer systems, electronic devices, software, or the Internet
- With an average connection speed of 26.7 mb/s, South Korea has the greatest Internet *connectivity* in the world.

evacuate
*to remove (persons or things) from a place, such as a disaster area, for reasons of safety or protection
- All the residents of the city were *evacuated* because of the impending hurricane.

publicly owned
*belonging to the citizens of a country and not to a private company
- *Publicly owned* utilities are non-profit, in contrast to investor-owned utilities, which operate for profit.

toll
*a payment or fee taken by the government for some right or privilege, such as for traveling along a road or over a bridge
- If you want to drive across the long bridge into Kobe, Japan, you'll have to pay a *toll* of $29.

user fee
*money charged for the use of something, especially a fee charged by a city government for the use of one of its services, such as garbage collection
- If you want to enter the national park, you'll have to pay a *user fee* of $15.

entity
*something having real or distinct existence, especially when considered as self-contained or independent of other things
- The Department of Agriculture is the main governmental *entity* responsible for supervising food safety.

traverse
*to extend across or over
- A long bridge *traverses* the river.

award a contract
*to choose the most preferable proposal for some enterprise and sign a contract for its fulfillment
- Azerbaijan *awarded the contract* for construction of Baku Olympic Stadium to a Korean firm.

concession
*a privilege or right granted by a government or controlling authority
- The government has granted a *concession* to a private company to operate the airport.

Let's Talk Business

Let's Talk Business

Discussion Points:

1. In your view, who should own the infrastructure in your country, the government or private companies?
2. Can you think of any situations in your country where private companies currently operate part of the infrastructure?
3. Has your country ever experienced a natural disaster that destroyed much of the infrastructure? What happened?
4. Do you have to pay tolls to cross bridges or drive down certain highways in your country?
5. Is it a wise idea for countries to pay billions of dollars to improve their infrastructure in order to host an international event?
6. How would you rate your country's Internet connectivity? Can you think of any ways that it could be improved?
7. How is the water supplied in your country? Do you think the water supply is reliable? Are you willing to drink tap water?

Current Hot Topic: Foreign Ownership of Infrastructure

Are there any circumstances under which a country might allow a foreign company to control some aspects of the country's infrastructure? This was a question faced in the U.S. in 2006 during the "Dubai Ports World" controversy. President George W. Bush supported offering contracts for port management to Dubai Ports World (DPW), a company based in the United Arab Emirates and under the direct control of the ruler of Dubai. If the U.S. agreed to the deal, DPW would manage the ports of New York, Philadelphia, Baltimore, Miami, and others. American politicians quickly objected to the deal, claiming that allowing a foreign power to control American ports would compromise U.S. port security. In face of mounting opposition, DPW sold its port operation contracts to an American firm that became known as Ports America. However, in 2017, a Turkish company sought to buy Ports America, which created the same sort of controversy that occurred in 2006.

For Further Discussion:

1. Would you support the concept of a foreign company managing such an important part of your country's infrastructure as port operations?
2. Have any foreign companies been involved in construction of infrastructure in your country, such as rail lines, airports, and subway systems?

Topic Preview:

If you had some money to invest, would you buy stocks in a tobacco or alcohol company? What about a company that owns casinos? If you knew a company produced weapons of war, would you invest in it, if you thought the company could make you rich? How important should "ethical investing" be to potential investors?

Dialogue:

Anthony: Lily, do you have any money invested in the stock market?

Lily: Yes, a little. I own shares in a mutual fund called Eventide Gilead Fund.

Anthony: Hmmm...I'm not familiar with it. What sort of fund is it?

Lily: The managers only invest in companies that create value, operate with integrity, and profit from ethical activities.

Anthony: What do you mean by "ethical activities"?

Lily: Well, the managers will not invest in any companies involved in gambling, tobacco, or alcohol.

Anthony: I see. Why did you choose that fund?

Lily: I'm a Christian, and I don't want my money supporting businesses that I think are evil.

Anthony: Okay. I respect your opinion on that. By the way, how is Eventide Gilead Fund performing?

Lily: Very well. Over the past five years, my investment has gained over 18%.

Anthony: Wow! That's very good. I have to look into this fund.

Lily: Yes, check it out. Just go to their website, and you can find all the information.

Ethical Investing

What is the best way for investors to maximize the return on their portfolio? Is it necessary to invest in companies that use unscrupulous means to make a profit? Many investors say yes. They are willing to invest in any company that can earn them money, even if that company is involved in products and practices that may be offensive to many people, including alcohol, tobacco, gambling, pornography, weapons, child labor, and products that damage the environment. Stocks in these types of companies are often called "sin stocks" that support "immoral products."

Investors in ethically questionable stocks often claim that they do not support the practices involved. These investors simply believe that certain companies will always be able to profit from people's bad habits. There is some evidence to support their view. For example, tobacco companies have traditionally fared well during economic slowdowns for one simple reason: smokers find that their bad habit is hard to break, especially during a faltering economy. In fact, alcohol and tobacco stocks usually outperform other stocks during a bear market.

While some investors are willing to make money off sin stocks, other investors are very careful about where they place their money. Such investors engage in what is known as "socially responsible investing" (SRI), most often through mutual funds that do not buy sin stocks, which promote products and activities the investors view as bad for society. How well does the performance of socially responsible mutual funds measure up compared to regular funds that invest in any kind of stocks? According to one index, the return on funds specializing in socially responsible investments between 1990 and 2015 was 10.46%. Over the same period, the S&P 500 produced a return of 9.93%. Thus, the approach of SRI produced a higher return over a 25-year period.

There is one drawback to investing in socially responsible funds. Such funds often have higher fees than regular funds. These higher fees are likely caused by the extensive research that mutual fund managers must undertake to find the most ethically responsible companies.

ISSUE 28 ETHICAL INVESTING

Vocabulary & Expressions:

return
*a yield or profit from labor, business, or investments; often used in the plural *returns*
- Mr. Lee invested in Microsoft early and received a great **return** on his investment.

portfolio
*the total number of investments held by an individual investor or by a financial organization
- It's wise to have a diversified **portfolio**, which means having investments in various companies.

unscrupulous means
*unethical methods; not following moral principles
- Every nation in the world recognizes that fraud and theft are **unscrupulous means** to gain money.

sin
*the deliberate violation of God's law or moral principles; any serious offence against a principle or standard
- Some people say that it's a **sin** to waste food.

immoral
*violating accepted moral principles; not conforming to accepted patterns of conduct
- Most schools consider it **immoral** for a teacher to date a student.

faltering
*moving in an unsteady, unstable manner
- Entertainment and hotel stocks were **faltering** during the recession.

bear market
*a stock market that is experiencing falling prices; the opposite of a *bull market*
- Investors become fearful and pessimistic during a **bear market**.

mutual funds
*investments of a company that issues shares to investors who allow the company to decide where to invest their money
- Many small investors put their money into **mutual funds** because they want their investments professionally managed and under government regulations.

measure up
*to reach a certain standard
- The cheap hotel did not **measure up** to the couple's expectations.

S&P 500
*the Standard & Poor's 500, a stock market index based on 500 large companies; considered one of the best indicators of the strength of the U.S. stock market
- The **S&P 500** lost 0.73% in value in 2015 but gained 9.54% in value in 2016.

drawback
*a hindrance or disadvantage; an undesirable aspect of something
- Married people often have problems, but living as a single person also has many **drawbacks**.

Let's Talk Business

Let's Talk Business

Discussion Points:

1. Do you think that "socially responsible investing" is important? Why or why not?
2. Would you rather buy shares in a mutual fund, which invests in many companies, or shares in just one strong company?
3. Would you ever invest in tobacco or alcohol companies? Why or why not?
4. Would you ever invest in food companies like Baskin Robbins and Dunkin' Donuts, even if you thought they contributed to the problem of obesity?
5. Is it ethical to make money off people's bad habits?
6. What kinds of companies would you never invest in?
7. Do you think it's important for a married couple to agree on an "investment philosophy"?

Current Hot Topic: Casino Stocks

For about a decade, casino stocks went up and down and did not reflect steady growth. However, some experts are predicting that casino stocks are well positioned for growth in the next few years. Companies like Wynn Resorts (WYNN), Las Vegas Sands (LVS), and MGM Resorts International (MGM) could earn great returns for investors. In spite of their potential for increasing one's wealth, casino stocks are still rejected by many investors because of religious and moral objections. Religious leaders have often opposed casino gambling because it is regarded as a sin that is based on greed. These leaders claim that the availability of gambling tempts people into gambling addiction and leads to poverty, corruption, suicide, prostitution, and other types of immorality. At the other end of the spectrum, some religious groups actually use bingo, blackjack, roulette, and poker to raise funds.

For Further Discussion:

1. Do you think that casino stocks are legitimate investments? Would you invest in casinos if you thought you could earn a lot of money?
2. Does your country allow casinos? Have they created any social problems?

We want to get married. If you permit us to tie the knot, we'll be able to produce cheaper and safer cars thanks to the combination of our advanced technologies.

I don't know who's right. But I have to decide when to buy my car. Should I buy it now or should I wait until the government lets them have their own way?

I hear that kind of plausible excuse all the time from corporations when they pursue their own interests. If we permit your marriage, consumers will see prices go up and services go down.

Topic Preview:

Why would one company want to buy another company? What advantages would they gain? What risks would they face? How does a company CEO or board of directors know when they should buy another company? Should companies be allowed to merge and form bigger companies without government approval?

Dialogue:

Joseph: Aubrey, I hear you're going on a European vacation this summer.

Aubrey: Yeah, that's right. I've been saving up for it for a long time.

Joseph: That sounds great. What airline are you flying?

Aubrey: American Airlines. They have good prices and good service.

Joseph: You don't like United Airlines? They have many flights to Europe.

Aubrey: True, but I refuse to fly United Airlines anymore.

Joseph: Why not?

Aubrey: After United Airlines completed their merger with Continental Airlines back in 2012, their service went downhill fast.

Joseph: I've heard a lot of people say that, actually.

Aubrey: Yeah, I wish that federal regulators had never approved that merger. Continental disappeared, and United got worse.

Mergers and Acquisitions

The term "mergers and acquisitions," or M&A, refers to transactions in which companies are combined. If one company buys or takes over another company, the transaction is known as an acquisition. The purchasing company is known as the acquirer, and the company that is purchased is known as the target. Companies merge because they want to break into new markets with new services, or they want to strengthen some aspect of their business that is weak.

The largest M&A of all time occurred in the year 2000. For months, the British mobile phone company Vodafone tried to buy the German telecom giant Mannesmann. The German company rejected Vodafone's first offer, and Vodafone had to nearly double its offer to $180 billion to complete the deal. In early 2000, Mannesmann agreed to the new offer, and Mannesmann was subsequently incorporated into the Vodafone Group. Unfortunately for Vodafone, the deal turned out to be a dud. In the following years, Vodafone had to write off tens of billions of dollars in losses.

An acquisition is also known as a "friendly takeover" because the target agrees to the takeover. In 2009, the Italian automaker Fiat took over Chrysler, a struggling American auto manufacturer, and created Fiat Chrysler Automobiles. In this type of takeover, Fiat is known as a white knight because it rescued Chrysler from its dire financial straits.

Some acquisitions are not friendly because the target does not want to be bought out. This type of transaction is known as a hostile takeover. In 2003, Oracle, an American computer technology corporation, began an attempt to take over PeopleSoft, a company that provided software to large businesses. PeopleSoft fought against the takeover but lost out in 2005, when Oracle managed to acquire the company for $10.3 billion. A month after the acquisition, Oracle laid off 6,000 of PeopleSoft's 11,000 employees.

Acquisitions are usually conducted only in cases of publicly traded companies. However, a private company sometimes takes over a public company, a transaction that is known as a "reverse takeover."

ISSUE 29 MERGERS AND ACQUISITIONS

Vocabulary & Expressions:

take over *to assume the control or management of a company, organization, or enterprise; noun form = takeover
- After the elderly supervisor retired, a new supervisor was chosen immediately to *take over* his position.

acquisition *the purchase of one business by another; from the verb *acquire*, meaning to come into possession or ownership of something
- In 2014, Facebook acquired WhatsApp for $19 billion, its largest *acquisition* ever.

break into *to begin some activity or enter a new area of activity
- In 1994, Starbucks' purchase of the Coffee Connection in Boston enabled it to *break into* new markets.

turn out to be *to come to be, to become ultimately
- The party *turned out to be* a great success.

dud *a device, person, or enterprise that ends up being a failure
- The cell phone that I bought turned out to be a *dud*.

write off *to consider a transaction as a loss against revenues
- During the financial crisis, many banks had to *write off* bad loans.

struggling *having difficulty to continue in a business, activity, etc.
- During the recession, Congress enacted many programs to help the *struggling* auto industry.

white knight *a company that comes to the rescue of another, especially in order to prevent a hostile takeover
- In 2008, Volkswagen acted as a *white knight* in acquiring Porsche, which was almost bankrupt.

dire financial straits *a desperate position of difficulty, distress, or need with respect to money
- After Mr. Brown lost his job, his family was in *dire financial straits* for months until he found a new job.

buy out *to purchase the ownership of a company
- In 2017, Amazon decided to *buy out* Whole Foods, so Amazon could enter the grocery market.

hostile takeover *an attempt to take over a company without the approval of the target company's management
- The largest *hostile takeover* occurred in the year 2000 when AOL acquired Time Warner for $164 billion.

publicly traded *a company that is owned by shareholders and whose shares are traded publicly
- You cannot buy shares in Dell, Inc. because it is a privately held company and is not *publicly traded*.

Let's Talk Business

Let's Talk Business

Discussion Points:

1. Do you think mergers and acquisitions are helpful to consumers? Why or why not?
2. Do you think mergers and acquisitions are helpful to employees of the companies involved? Why or why not?
3. What is the largest M&A that you have heard about in your country? Was it beneficial to both companies?
4. If you were the CEO of a company being targeted for a hostile takeover, what would you do?
5. Can you think of any companies that do not exist anymore because they were taken over by another company?
6. Can you think of two companies in your country that would be ideal companies to merge?
7. Can you think of any large companies in your country that are in such dire financial straits that they would welcome a takeover?

Current Hot Topic: Government Control of Mergers and Acquisitions

In 2001, the U.S. Justice Department rejected a merger of United Airlines and US Airways on the grounds that the merger would reduce consumer choices and lead to higher airfares. However, in recent years, the Justice Department has taken a different view of mergers. They allowed the merger of Delta and Northwest in 2008 and the merger of United Airlines and Continental in 2010. Then in 2013, they allowed American Airlines and US Airways to merge, forming the largest airline in the U.S. All of these mergers mean that the U.S. is now left with just three major air carriers. With fewer air carriers, passengers have fewer options and face increasing fares and fees. When Hillary Clinton campaigned for the presidency in 2016, she promised, "As president, I will appoint tough, independent authorities to scrutinize mergers and acquisitions, so the big don't keep getting bigger and bigger."

For Further Discussion:

1. Do you think it was a mistake for the U.S. Justice Department to allow so many airlines to merge? Should governments exercise more control over mergers and acquisitions?
2. Do you think your government does a good job of regulating mergers and acquisitions?

British Queen: We've decided to say goodbye to the EU. We want to have a good relationship with the United States, including a new FTA.

Trump: No problem. We've been good friends for a long time. Then why did you decide to go for Brexit?

British Queen: Just between you and me, we did some calculations and concluded that we'd better get out of it.

Trump: I see. Well, wait a while. I'll get back to you after I do some calculations about our relationship.

Topic Preview:

Why would so many European countries give up their traditional laws and currency and agree to conform to the rules of the European Union? What advantages do EU member states gain by being part of the organization? Is it possible for members to withdraw from the union? What consequences might ex-members face?

Dialogue:

Lillian: John, you're from the U.K., right?

John: Yes, that's correct.

Lillian: If you don't mind me asking, did you support withdrawing the U.K. from the European Union?

John: No, I don't mind you asking, and no, I did not support Brexit. I was very upset about it.

Lillian: Why do you think British voters chose to leave the EU?

John: Some politicians stirred up nationalist sentiment, especially among older people.

Lillian: I see. So most young people did not support Brexit?

John: No, they didn't. They want easy access to travel, education, and jobs throughout the EU.

Lillian: What do you think will happen in the future?

John: I think that my fellow British citizens will eventually regret their decision to leave the EU, especially when they see that our economy is not doing as well as that of the EU.

The European Union

In 1957, six European countries signed the Treaty of Rome, which created the European Economic Community (EEC), which later became known simply as the European Union, or EU. The EU now embraces 28 member states, including its most recent member, Croatia, which joined in 2013. The total population of the EU now surpasses 510 million, representing about 7% of the world population. In 2012, the EU received the Nobel Peace Prize for contributing "to the advancement of peace and reconciliation, democracy, and human rights in Europe."

In 2002, the EU introduced the euro, which replaced 12 national currencies and created the Eurozone. Later, seven additional countries adopted the currency. The euro is now the second largest reserve currency in the world, second only to the U.S. dollar. As of January 2017, the total value of euro notes and coins in circulation exceeded €1.1 trillion, which surpassed the value of U.S. dollars in circulation. A total of nine EU members do not use the euro.

When countries join the EU, it is obvious that one of their primary reasons is to take advantage of the combined economic clout of such a large confederation. The EU, considered as a whole, has certainly achieved economic prominence. In 2014, the EU had a combined GDP of $18.6 trillion, which presented a 20% share of the global GDP, when viewed by purchasing power parity (PPP). EU member states own about 30% of the $223 trillion global wealth, the largest share of any one group. Of the 500 largest corporations in the world, 161 have their headquarters in the EU. The EU has thrown its weight around, signing numerous free trade agreements, including ones with Chile (2002), South Korea (2010), and Ukraine (2014).

Unfortunately, much of the wealth of the EU is concentrated in the richest countries. In 2017, citizens of Denmark enjoyed a monthly income of €3,095, the highest in the EU. However, the citizens of 12 EU countries had an average monthly income of less than €1,000, including Bulgaria at the bottom with a mere €333.

ISSUE 30 THE EUROPEAN UNION

Vocabulary & Expressions:

embrace
*to include or contain
- An encyclopedia *embraces* thousands of articles on various subjects.

Eurozone
*a monetary union of 19 of the 28 EU member states that have adopted the euro as their sole common currency; also known as *the euro area*
- Sweden is a member of the EU but not of the *Eurozone*.

adopt
*to accept, take up, or start to follow an idea, method, or course of action
- The metric system has been *adopted* by every country except the U.S., Liberia, and Myanmar.

reserve currency
*an international currency that is held in large quantities by governments as part of their foreign exchange reserves and which is used in international transactions
- The U.S. dollar is considered the world's dominant *reserve currency*.

note
*a promissory monetary note issued and printed by a central bank, serving as money; also known as *bank note* (or *banknote*), *paper money*, or *bill*
- U.S. *notes* are issued in seven denominations: $1, $2, $5, $10, $20, $50, and $100.

in circulation
*currently in use and not stored in reserves
- The U.S. $2-bill is rare *in circulation*, but there are millions stored in banks.

clout
*power or influence, especially in political and financial matters
- Steven Spielberg has a lot of *clout* in Hollywood.

confederation
*a group of nations or governments that delegate some power to a central authority but retain considerable independence for themselves
- Canada is officially a *confederation* of ten provinces and three territories.

purchasing power parity
*an economic theory that states the following: the real exchange rate between two currencies is equal to the ratio of the currencies' respective purchasing power
- If a McDonald's Big Mac costs the same in two countries (after exchanging currency), then those two countries are said to have *purchasing power parity*.

throw one's weight around
*to use one's power and influence, especially to make some personal gain
- The politician tried to *throw his weight around* to get a job for his son.

mere
*being no more or no better than something specified; often used to emphasize how small or insignificant someone or something is
- Child labor is immoral; we cannot expect *mere* children to work like adults.

Let's Talk Business

Discussion Points:

1. Why are some countries in the EU very rich and others very poor? Should the EU seek to make all the countries equal in per capita income?
2. Do you think the EU deserved to receive the Nobel Peace Prize? Why or why not?
3. Does your country have a free trade agreement with the EU? If so, do you think the agreement is beneficial?
4. Do you think the euro will ever replace the dollar as the leading reserve currency?
5. What currencies does your country use mainly for its foreign reserves? Should it make any adjustments?
6. Have you ever compared prices of the same item in your country and another country (e.g., a McDonald's Big Mac or a Starbucks latte)? Was there purchasing power parity between the two countries?
7. Would you like to see your country join a confederation like the EU? Would you be willing to give up your local currency and adopt a unified currency?

Current Hot Topic: Effects of Brexit

On June 23, 2016, a slight majority of British voters voted for the United Kingdom to leave the European Union, an event known as Brexit. Those who argued for leaving the EU claimed that the U.K. had lost control of its own laws and immigration policies. Thus, the supporters of Brexit were somewhat nationalistic. They did not like the idea of being subject to EU laws that allowed any EU citizen to cross freely into the U.K. to live and work. Arguments against Brexit were concerned about the economic impact of leaving. While a member of the EU, the U.K. could freely trade with other member states. When the U.K. is no longer a member of the EU, it will have to negotiate free trade agreements with individual EU members, a process that could take years. The simple fact is that no one knows exactly what the economic impact of Brexit will be on the U.K. Negotiations for the withdrawal started in June 2017, and the U.K. is expected to leave the EU on March 29, 2019.

For Further Discussion:

1. Do you think Brexit will help or hurt the United Kingdom? If you were a British citizen, would you have voted to remain in the EU or to leave?
2. Do you think that other countries will soon leave the EU (e.g., France, Italy, Poland, and the Netherlands)? Why or why not?

APPENDIX

Openers for Your Discussion!

다음은 1:1 대화나 집단토론에서 자주 쓰이는 표현 (특히 처음 시작할 때의 표현을 중심으로)을 정리해 놓은 것입니다.

1) 모르는 사람에게 무엇인가를 묻기 위해 접근해서 이야기를 걸 때	Pardon me Sorry May I interrupt for a moment?	Excuse me Pardon me for interrupting, but
2) 집단 토론 중에 갑자기 지적할 문제가 생겨 말을 끊고 나올 때	Sorry, but May I add something? May I ask a question? I'd like to comment on that I have a point here	I might add here May I say something here? Excuse me for interrupting, but I'd like to say something
3) 원래의 주제로 다시 돌아갈 때	Anyway To return to To get back to Going back to What were we talking about?	In anycase Returning to Let's get back to Where was I?
4) 누군가에게 무엇을 물어볼 때	I'd like to know Could you tell me Do you know	I'm interested in Could I ask Do you happen to know
5) 주저하거나 망설임을 나타낼 때	Well Now You know	Look You see Listen
6) 일의 순서를 나열할 때	First First of all Secondly Then So Before you finish At the end As the last thing	To begin with Next After that So then Finally

APPENDIX

7) 중요한 점을 부각 시킬 때	First of all The most important thing is	The main thing is Primarily
8) 중요한 문제점을 지적할 때	The trouble is Don't forget that The awful thing is	The problem is The real problem is
9) 놀랄만한 사실을 이야기할 때	Do you realize that Believe it or not It may sound strange (or funny), but Strangely enough	Surprisingly You may not believe this, but
10) 새로운 사실을 이야기할 때	Guess what! Do you know what?	I've got news for you! You won't believe this, but
11) 일반적인 사실을 이야기할 때	Generally As a rule usually On the average	By and large Normally Typically
12) 상대방에게 즐겁지 않은 사실을 이야기 하고자 할 때	Actually To tell the truth To be blunt	But frankly To be honest
13) 현실적인 이야기를 하고자 할 때	To be honest with you Now be realistic	Let's face it
14) 이야기의 주제를 바꿀 때	Speaking of By the way I just thought of something	That reminds me Before I forget
15) 자기 의견을 이야기할 때	I think In my opinion I personally think I suspect I'm almost positive	I imagine In my estimation To my mind I'm pretty sure I have reason to believe
16) 자기 확신을 이야기할 때	I strongly believe I'm convinced Without a doubt	I'm positive Undoubtedly

APPENDIX

17) 개인적인 상황을 이야기할 때	In my case Personally, I'm more interested in	What I'm concerned with is For my own part
18) 소문 따위의 비밀스런 이야기를 하고자 할 때	I've heard Just between you and me I hear they say	They say Rumor has it
19) 어떤 제안을 하고자 할 때	Why don't you If I were you, I would Perhaps you could Try May I make a suggestion	I suggest you Why not How about I have an idea
20) 어떤 계획에 대하여 이야기 하고자 할 때	I'm planning to Our plan is to What we have in mind is What we plan to do is	What I'm planning to do is We are thinking of Our scheme is
21) 어떤 특정한 포인트에 대해 설명하고자 할 대	Regarding As far as (something) is concerned Where (something) is concerned When it comes to (something) In that respect On that point	Concerning As far as that goes In that instance
22) 특정한 상황에 대해 의견을 말할 때	In a case like this In a situation like this In this type of situation	In this case In such a situation In this instance
23) 어떤 특정한 포인트를 강조할 때	That's just the point But the point is This raises a problem But the problem with that is	But the question is But the real question is This raises a question
24) 특정한 포인트를 추가할 때	Also In addition In other respect Perhaps I should mention Not to mention the fact that Not only that, but	And another thing What's more I might add I almost forgot Plus the fact that

APPENDIX

25) 이유를 설명할 때	The reason why Owing to Because Since	The main reason why Due to Because of
26) 제시된 이유에 대한 부연설명을 할 때	For this reason Owing to this This is why That's why Therefore As a result Thus	On account of this Because of this This is the reason why That's the reason why So Consequently
27) 즉각적인 대답 보다는 약간 망설임을 나타낼 때	Well, uhm Let's put it this way	Well, let's see I'll have to think about that
28) 자기 자신의 의견 (또는 의미)을 분명히 할 때	What I mean is What I'm saying is Don't get me wrong Don't misunderstand me (on this point) Let me put it another way What I really said You must have misunderstood me Let's get this straight, I said	What I meant was What I'm trying to say is That's not what I said
29) 무엇인가를 거절할 때	I don't care for I'm not going to I don't like What I can't stand is I'm not really interested in I don't need I don't have the time to I'm perfectly satisfied with I'd prefer	I can't stand This isn't my idea of I can't take I'm not worried about I have no use for I'm not concerned with I'd rather
30) 질문하고 무엇인가를 제안할 때	I wonder why Are you serious when you say Why do you	Do you really think (or believe) Isn't it true that Do you mean to say

APPENDIX

	Don't you think (or say, or agree)	Wouldn't it be better
	Wouldn't it be a good idea	Why don't you
	I wonder if	
31) 설명을 요구할 때	Can you explain why	I wonder why
	I don't understand why	I keep wondering why
	Why is it that	Why do you think
	What do you mean by	
	What do you have in mind (with)	
32) 어떤 계획에 대해 유보적인 입장을 취할 때	I doubt	I'm afraid
	I don't know if	But the problem is
	Yes, but	Possibly, but
	Sure, but	That's a good idea, but
	I'd love to, but	That would be great, except
	That may be so, but	Yes, but the question is
	I don't see advantage in	What I'm worried about is
	What I'm concerned about is	What I'm afraid of is
	What bothers me is	What I don't like is
	One drawback is	
33) 어떤 점을 고려하라고 할 때	Considering	Seeing
	Taking into account	Remembering
	If you remember	Keeping in mind
	Allowing for the fact	When you consider
	All things considered	
34) 다른 대안이 없어 굴복할 때	If there's no other way	If there's no alternative
	If that's so	
	Well, under those circumstances	
35) 빈도(Frequency)를 나타낼 때	Generally	In general
	As a rule	Mostly
	Ordinarily	As a general rule
	Usually	Most of the time
	Again and again	Time and again
	Once in a while	Every so often
	From time to time	Every now and then

APPENDIX

36) 예외를 지적할 때	There are exceptions, of course One should mention, of course An exception to that is, of course This does not include With the exception of (that) Except that One exception is But what about But think of
37) 예를 들고자 할 때	For example For instance Take for example A classic example of this is For one thing To give you an idea To illustrate my point Just as an example As an illustration
38) 요약 및 결론을 이야기할 때	To make a long story short So in short So you see So finally So All in all In the end To conclude To sum up To summarize Summing up To put it into a few words To put it in a nutshell In a nutshell In brief
39) 동의를 나타낼 때	That's right Right Okay Correct Yes Exactly I agree (with you) You're right That's true I know I guess so That's just what I was thinking. That's exactly what I was thinking. I couldn't agree with you more. That's exactly what I think. I feel the same way. My feelings exactly. I'll say You can say that again. That's a good point. I see your point.
40) 반대를 나타낼 때	That's ridiculous Are you kidding? Aw, come on! What do you mean? What!

APPENDIX

	I don't believe it	No, definitely not
	Are you pulling my leg?	That doesn't fit.
	I disagree	I don't agree
	I don't think so	I don't think that's fair
	I'm not sure	I hate to disagree with you, but
41) 불행한 사건에 대해 반응할 때	Oh no	That's too bad
	What a pity	What a shame
	What a nuisance	Poor you
	How awful	How terrible
	That must have been awful	I'm sorry to hear that
	Oh, my God	
42) 예상했던(당연한) 불행한 결과에 대한 반응	It's your own fault	Someday you'll learn
	That'll teach you	Serves you right
	What else did you expect?	
43) 상대방의 말에 흥미를 보일 때	Right	Okay
	Yeah	Yes?
	And?	Well?
	Really?	And then?
	And so?	Mh-hmm
	Uh-huh	
44) 반복을 요청할 때	Pardon me?	I beg your pardon?
	Could you say that again?	
	Would you repeat that, please?	
	Sorry?	
	Would you mind repeating that?	You lost me there
	I didn't catch that last part.	What's that again?
	Sorry, I don't follow you.	I'm lost.
	I didn't get that.	
45) 전화상에서 상대방에게 반복을 요구할 때	Sorry, what did you say?	Pardon?
	I'm sorry I didn't understand that.	
	Do you mind repeating that?	
	Can you repeat that for me, please?	
	Sorry?	

46) 상대방의 이해정도를 확인할 때	Are you following me? Is that clear? Are you coming along fine? Got it?	Are you with me? Okay so far? Do you understand so far? Right?
47) 상대방의 칭찬에 대한 답을 할 때	Oh, thank you Kind of you to say that Do you really think so? I'm flattered. That's nice to hear	Oh, thanks That's very kind of you Thanks, I needed that. Oh, I'm glad you think so.
48) 더이상 이야기할 시간이 없을 때	Sorry, I've got to go I must be going I hope you don't mind, but	I have to run Would you excuse me, please?
49) 전화한 사람이 끊을려고 할 때	I'd better let you go I know you are busy, so I'll let you go It's been good talking to you	Thanks for your time
50) 전화 받은 사람이 끊을려고 할 때	Well, thanks for calling I'm afraid I don't have time to talk I appreciate your calling	

DISCUSSION TEXTBOOKS
FROM LIS KOREA

중고급 어린이들을 위한 독창적인 영어교재

New Children's Talk (1), (2), (3)

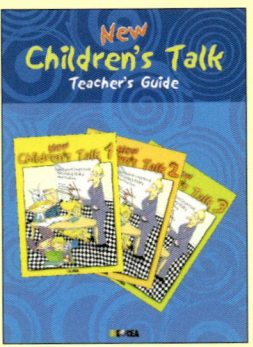

교사용

New Children's Talk (TG)

- 일상생활에서 벌어지는 상황들을 다양한 포맷에 맞추어서 많은 Speaking Chance를 제공합니다.
- 암기 위주의 영어가 아니라 자기 의견을 만들어 낼 수 있는 포맷들을 제공합니다.

청소년의 세계와 그들의 생각 관심사들을 토론으로

Chat Room for Teens (1)(2)(3)

- New Children's Talk를 배운 학생들이 Teen Talk를 쉽게 익힐 수 있는 선행학습교재로 사용할 수 있도록 구성
- 학습의 재미와 능률을 높이기 위해 다양한 그림들과 그것들을 바탕으로 한 토론들 그리고 실제 많은 상황에서 발생하는 대화들과 수많은 지문들을 바탕으로 토론의 다양성을 확보

DISCUSSION TEXTBOOKS
FROM LIS KOREA

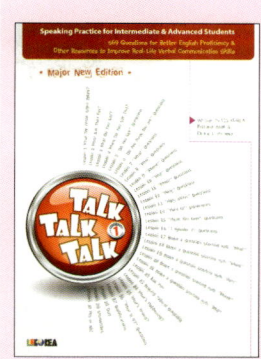 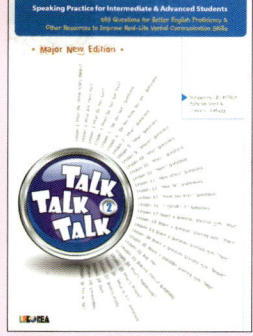

자유토론을 위한 훈련과정
Talk Talk Talk (1), (2)

- Express Yourself / Let's Talk / What Do You Think? 과정을 무리 없이 이수하기 위한 예비단계로서 자유토론에 대비하기 위한 많은 훈련과정을 포함하고 있다.
- 여러 상황에 맞는 다양한 질문을 학생들에게 던짐으로써 질문과 응답들의 패턴을 이해하고 습득하게 하고자 했다.
- Express Yourself / Let's Talk / What Do You Think?의 주요 훈련 목표 중 하나인 어떤 영어 단어나 문장을 토론자 스스로 다시 설명하는 훈련에 중점을 두었다.

Talk Talk Talk의 선생님 교재
Teacher's Guide for Talk Talk Talk 1&2

- 기존에 출간 되었던 당사의 교재 Talk Talk Talk 1, 2의 선생님 교재로 출간 되었습니다.
- Talk Talk Talk 1, 2에 나왔던 모든 질문에 대한 정확한 답변과 필요한 경우 찬반 의견들이 모두 제시되어있습니다.

DISCUSSION TEXTBOOKS
FROM LIS KOREA

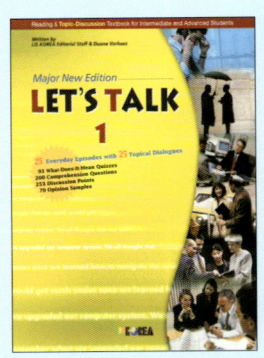 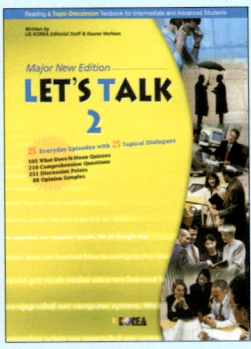

중고급 토론교재의 결정판
LET'S TALK! (1), (2)

- 실생활과 아주 밀접하고 분명한 의견 대립이 나올 수 있는 주제를 선정 고급 토론 영어를 위한 기초를 가질 수 있도록 구성.
- 토론 영어의 기초 단계인 영어로 설명하는 힘을 길러주기 위해 "What Does It Mean?"을 삽입.

- Question에서는 제시된 주제에 대한 이해력 측정뿐만 아니라 한 주제에 대한 깊이 있는 토론에 대비하는 힘을 길러 주고자 했다.
- Discussion Points에서는 주어진 주제에 대한 토론 포인트는 물론이고 그와 연관된 많은 주제 제공
- Opinion Samples에서는 학습자들이 주어진 주제에 대해 토론을 준비할 수 있도록 만은 찬반 의견과 참고 의견들을 제시하고 있다.
- 어려운 표현이나 Idiomatic Expressions에 대해 각주에 충분한 영어 설명을 달아 학습자들로 하여금 이해가 쉽도록 하였다.

중급자들을 위한 토론교재
Speak Your Mind (1), (2)

- 일상적이며 쉬운 주제들을 선정하여 간결하게 정리했음.
- 대표 주제에 대한 질문과 대답을 여론조사 형식으로 꾸며 독자들이 쉽게 주제에 접근할 수 있도록 했음.
- 모든 주제들에 찬반 의견을 달아 독자들의 다양한 의견을 접할 수 있도록 했음.

DISCUSSION TEXTBOOKS
FROM LIS KOREA

청소년을 위한 토론교재
New Teen Talk (1), (2)

- 청소년 토론교재의 최고 높은 단계의 교재로서 각 권 15개의 이슈 속에 500개 이상의 토론주제를 제시합니다.
- 각 권에 포함된 9개의 포맷은 (What Does It Mean?/Comprehension/Teen Talk/Opinion Samples/Dialog/Read & Discuss/Pictures Talk/What's Your Advice?/Synopsis/) 각각의 특징에 맞는 다양하고 흥미로운 토론 주제를 제공합니다.

토론교재의 베스트셀러
EXPRESS YOURSELF (1), (2), (3)
3rd Edition

- 토론 영어교재의 베스트셀러 Express Yourself 1/2/3 시리즈가 새롭게 출간되었습니다. 각 권 15개의 이슈를 깊이 있게 다루고 있으며, 다양한 토론주제와 Opinion Samples를 제공하고, 연관 dialog를 첨부하여 주제에 대한 이해력을 배가 시켰습니다.
- Points to Ponder 섹션에서는 다양한 의견들이 나올 수 있는 주제를 제시하여 다양한 토론이 되도록 했습니다.
- 토론주제와 연결되는 다양한 수백 개의 그림과 더불어 캡션을 덧붙여서 미국영어의 재미와 아름다움을 느끼도록 하였습니다.

DISCUSSION TEXTBOOKS
FROM LIS KOREA

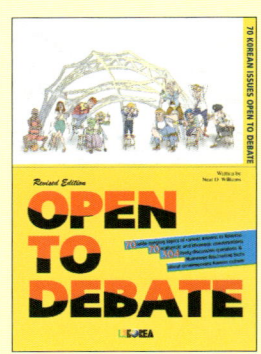 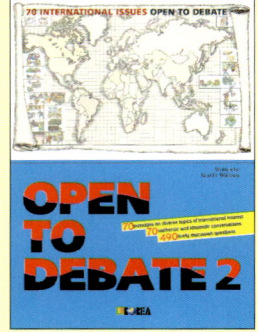

70개의 국내/국제 쟁점들로 구성된 영어토론 교재
Open To Debate (1), (2)

- 현 한국 및 국제사회에서 문제 되고 있는 70개의 이슈를 선정하여 300개가 넘는 작은 토론 주제를 제공해줍니다.
- 각 이슈의 도입 부분에 다이얼로그를 제공하여 주제에 대한 흥미를 더해줍니다.
- 한국 사회의 토론 이슈를 영어로 살펴볼 수 있는 최적의 교재입니다.

설명간결한 형식의 새로운 토론교재
Express Yourself Directly (1), (2)

- Pictures Talk 섹션에서는 큰 주제에 대한 warm-up 주제들을 선정하여 그림과 함께 제시하여 본 주제에 쉽게 접근할 수 있도록 했습니다.
- Express Yourself Directly 섹션에서는 Pictures Talk 섹션에서 다루지 않은 좀 더 깊은 주제를 선정하여 심도 있는 토론이 되도록 했습니다.
- Let's Talk Funny 섹션에서는 본 주제와 관련있는 재미 있는 이야기를 실어 가벼운 토론과 함께 긴장을 풀도록 했습니다.
- What Does It Mean?에서는 본 주제와 관련된 Food For Thought를 제공하여 학습자들이 자유롭게 토론 할 수 있도록 했으면 다양한 의견이 나올 수 있는 문구들을 제시하였습니다.
- 마지막으로 Synopsis에서는 (전체 400의 그림으로 구성) 각 그림에 대한 설명을 영어로 명쾌하게 제시하여 학습자가 주제에 대한 최종 복습을 할 수 있도록 했습니다.

DISCUSSION TEXTBOOKS
FROM LIS KOREA

 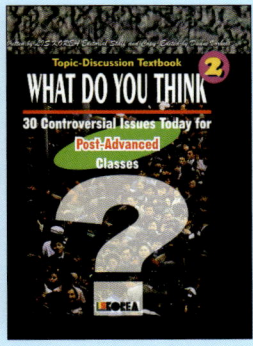

고급 토론 교재의 완결판
What Do You Think? (1), (2)

- Let's talk를 끝낸 학습자들이 좀 더 시사적이며 깊이 있는 문제들에 대해 토론할 수 있도록 구성
- 토론 영어의 기초단계인 영어로 설명하는 힘을 길러주기 위해 What Does It Mean?을 삽입

- Question에서는 제시된 주제에 대해 이해력 측정뿐만 아니라 한 주제에 대한 깊이 있는 토론에 대비하는 힘을 길러 주고자 했다.
- What Do You Think?에서는 주어진 주제에 대한 토론 포인트는 물론이고 그와 연관된 많은 주제 제공
- Opinion Samples에서는 학습자들이 주어진 주제에 대해 토론을 준비할 수 있도록 만은 찬반 의견과 참고 의견들을 제시하고 있다.
- 어려운 표현이나 Idiomatic Expressions에 대해 각주에 충분한 영어 설명을 달아 학습지들로 하여금 이해가 쉽도록 하였다.

재미있는 창작 이야기로 토론의 즐거움을
LET'S TALK FUNNY

- 70개의 재미있는 창작 이야기가 수백 개의 토론 이슈와 어우러져 독자들에게 재미있게 영어로 토론할 수 있는 기회를 제공합니다.
- 또한, 우리 생활에 감추어져 있던 또 다른 50개의 Thinking Points를 제공하여 발상을 전환할 수 있는 계기가 되도록 했습니다.

― Major New Edition ―
Let's Talk BUSINESS

초판 1쇄 인쇄 : 2019년 11월 1일 인쇄
초판 1쇄 발행 : 2019년 11월 5일 발행
지 은 이 : Neal D. Williams
펴 낸 곳 : (도서출판) 리스코리아
펴 낸 이 : 조은예
등   록 : 남양주 제 399-2011-000003호
전   화 : (0502) 423-7947
일러스트레이터 : 김나나
편 집 디 자 인 : 이명금, 최윤경
인   쇄 : (주)미광원색사

www.liskorea.com

All rights reserved. No part of this book may be
reproduced, stored in a retrieval system, or
transmitted in any form or by any means, electronic,
mechanical, photocopying, recording or otherwise,
without the prior permission in writing of the Publisher.

— It's been three years since you graduated from college, and you still don't have any job. What's wrong?
— I've been looking for jobs that suit me, but I can't find one.
— What kind of job do you want?
— I don't want a six-digit salary job, but my working time should be FLEXIBLE. So I can work when I feel okay but stay home when I don't.

Poor: You have a moral responsibility to help the poor.
Rich: Why?
Poor: You're getting richer while we're getting poorer. We can't help it.
Rich: Your laziness is the problem! If you work hard, you can make lots of money and live like us.
Poor: You're lying! Don't you see I work from sunrise to sunset every day on the street begging for pennies?

They obviously have very different views of what work is.

As a last resort, earthmen finally started traveling to space. Their mission is to capture the sun and moon and sell them to the ETs to pay off their debt. They think they'll have no problem capturing the moon, but the sun is different because it is still burning. So they have prepared a big fire extinguisher. If their mission is accomplished successfully, all debt problems on Earth will be resolved.

Importer: Make the US dollar much stronger, so we can import more goods and have stabilized prices.

Exporter: Make the US dollar much weaker, so we can export more goods to other countries, and manufacturers will employ more workers.

They both have a point. Maybe we should just flip a coin.